SPIRITUAL PORTALS

Other books by Nora D'Ecclesis…

Mastering Tranquility: Developing Powerful Stress Management Skills

Tranquil Seas: Applying Guided Visualization

Reiki Roundtable

The Retro Budget Prescription: Skillful Personal Planning

I'm So Busy! Efficient Time Management

Lock Your Door: Passwords, PINS & Hackers

Haiku: Natures Meditation

Adult Coloring: Be a Kid Again!

Equanimity & Gratitude

Tick-Borne: Questing to Vampire

Twin Flame: A Novella

Spiritual Portals

A Historical Perspective

by Nora D'Ecclesis

Published by Renaissance Presentations, LLC
King of Prussia, PA

ISBN-13: 978-1-7330201-0-7
ISBN-10: 1-7330201-0-1

1st Edition: May, 2019

Dedication

Spiritual Portals is dedicated to my former classmate and lifelong friend, Joan. We had the good fortune of becoming friends in middle school and then attended college and graduate school at the same university. As alumnae we now attend college homecoming and high school reunions. Joan has a unique understanding of global spiritual traditions from her extensive international travel. She has shared her enhanced spiritual discoveries over the years and enjoyed my work as a spiritual lecturer at retreats.

While working in Hong Kong, Joan climbed the 268 steps to see the "Big Buddha" Tian Tan, and visited "Reclining Buddha" in Bangkok, Thailand. The mystical sounds of the monks chanting have created her passion for both Gregorian and Buddhist chanting music. Joan has stood where Christ was crucified, put her note in the Wailing Wall, and walked the Great Wall of China.

Joan epitomizes how walking through spiritual portals in her global travels created her loving respect and knowledge of religions of the world and their traditions.

Deep bows to my amazingly spiritual friend Joan.

May I become at all times, both now and forever,

A protector for those without protection,

A guide for those who have lost their way,

A ship for those with oceans to cross,

A bridge for those with rivers to cross,

A sanctuary for those in danger,

A lamp for those without light,

A place of refuge for those who lack shelter,

And a servant to all in need.

by Shantideva,
an 8th century Indian Buddhist monk

SPIRITUAL PORTALS

Spirituality is a uniquely individual experience resulting from an introspective assessment of the moral, ethical and compassionate components of our lives. It includes the non-materialistic aspects of life. Exploring one's spirituality is a transformative process of the core need for solitude and includes ethical and moral choices. A human's true self experiences personal growth during the contemplative process usually resulting in a more compassionate existence for themselves and others who they interact with during their lifetime.

Currently one-third of Americans define themselves as spiritual, not religious. Spiritual but not religious (SBNR) is an acronym used to describe this thirty percent. There are two perspectives defining spirituality: traditional and new age. In the 15th Century the traditional concept of spirituality taught that religion was the path to personal growth by working toward becoming closer to the image of God. Kabbalah as a school of thought of Judaism is a profoundly spiritual quest toward answering many of the ontological questions that exist. The study of being or ontology is explored by Islamic Sufism as a mystical spirituality. According to Sufi teacher Anmadibn Ajiba "a science through which one can know how to travel into the presence of the Divine, purify one's inner self and beautify it with a variety of praiseworthy traits," in his book *The Principles of Sufism*. In early Christianity spirituality was considered as a process to reform in the image of God and living out of a personal act of faith in the study of the Holy Spirit.

After World War II in America, theistic and spiritual disconnected. It became a unique experience rather than in the past, everyone approached a more spiritual path by means of doctrines from organized religions. It is hoped that this book will provide an in depth and comprehensive view to the techniques, methodology and most importantly the history of modalities selected to bring the reader toward a more spiritual existence without or in combination with faith-based religions. The spiritual component to our daily lives is always a transformative path intended to create change as a result of spiritual practice.

It is with great respect to the giants who have examined the adult stages of life from Carl Jung to Wayne Dyer that in this composite of their theories we explore how to move from the teen age years to the end of life in a more spiritual experience. In exploring the Athlete or Vanity Stage there is room to believe that many adolescents skip it entirely or move quickly to the more advanced levels. The vanity phase consists of the ultimate narcissism when appearances and good looks in trendy appropriate attire is all that matters. The pecking order forms as many move quickly up to higher status by virtue of materialistic means and values clarification from their peers or equally materialistic parents. Many however can be seen spending free time working at service in soup kitchens, cleaning the local communities of litter or giving compassionately of their energies in various endeavors. They are the youngsters who probably also never bullied anyone in their high school cafeterias. What if teaching or learning the alternatives of a more spiritual existence at this early stage could result in a more fully self-actualized human with better quality and quantity of life? At the very least there would be choices and introspection. The next stage is known as warrior and for good reason, it is similar to approaching a competitive battlefield. As most adolescents advance to the more competitive phase, they immerse themselves in a dog-eat-dog style of aggressive competition, resulting in a combative style of achieving the goals and jobs complete with latest sports car and zip code for definition of their status. The shift goes from physical attributes to materialistic conquest. This continues normally during the years of raising a family and well into adulthood for perhaps twenty years after adolescence. Toward the end of this stage there is something casually referred to as a mid-life crisis when people are in need of finding themselves, as many say or simply realizing there must be more to life.

The statesman is an interesting stage and comes with the gestalt that maybe it might be time to give back to humanity and become the all-knowing caring individual. There is a more compassionate attempt to achieve a better way of life. Generally this is done without expectation of reciprocity so checks are written to fund the soup kitchen and donations and charitable contributions are made. This is classically a stage after financial freedom is secured and not one found in early teenage years. Many of the stages are interchangeable but not this one which is where humans from all walks of life from the middle class to billionaires for the most part fixate and remain.

The final stage is the more self-actualized enlightened one and usually presents toward the end of one's life on this earth. It is a spiritual end for most after ninety years old and almost all on their death bed. It is a place of realizing the insignificance of accomplishments and letting go of any control they thought they had.

The spiritual portals are some of the many available in the 21st Century some of which will resonate with the reader and become part of daily life regimen.

YOGA

The forms of mind and body exercise such as yoga integrate mood and body movement with a sense of spirituality and connection with nature. They can be performed at lower intensities inclusive of a wide range of functional abilities. Yoga requires no equipment and can be performed at home. The mindful awareness as a component involved in doing yoga can make this type of activity a complement to a meditation or an alternative to meditation for those who prefer higher levels of activity when trying to focus the mind.

Yoga is a spiritual union between the mind and body. The six branches of yoga: Inana, Karma, Mantra, Tantra, Raja and Hatha all have origins in Hindu practice, teaching discernment, a toned body and asanas. Hindu spiritual practice explores sattua, rajas and tamas through guna, which loosely translated means the congenital or innate nature of including all the psychological components of a human being. In the early nineteenth Century Ralph Waldo Emerson's transcendentalists formulated a universal spirituality with God looking out for all. This occurred as a result of the transcendentalists reading the Hindu texts.

One branch of yoga called Hatha, has spawned several variations of what we have commonly come to know in the western hemisphere as yoga practice. The postures or asanas involve many physical movements such as bending and twisting, performed standing seated or lying on the floor. Combined with controlled breathing and meditative awareness these movements challenge balance flexibility and muscular endurance.

Yogic breathing Pranayama is used in conjunction with each posture to promote further connection between mind and body. Whether the objective is relaxation, muscle toning, spiritual evolution or simply flexibility a yoga practice can be customized to fit the needs of just about anyone at any age.

Nadi Shodhana or alternate nostril breathing prepares us for deeper spiritual meditation by balancing the right and left hemispheres of the brain and reducing stress. The technique can be done in steps:

Sit in a meditative posture on a Zafu/Zabutan.

Place the right thumb to close the right nostril and inhale to a count of four slowly through the left nostril, then close off the left nostril with the ring finger. Open and exhale slowly through the right nostril to a count of eight.

Now, exhale through the right open nostril to a count of four closing it at that point with your thumb. Open and exhale to a count of eight through left nostril.

Repeat 3x and return to your normal breathing patterns.

The word yoga means to join, the individual self with the higher spiritual consciousness. The following applied theory is example of how to start.

APPLIED THEORY

Tree Pose — or Vriksasana — is a classically Hatha Yoga meditative pose: Stand tall in Tadasana with your arms at your side then shift weight to one leg. Place the left foot firmly on the ground. Bend the right knee as it is raised up on the left inner thigh with head to toe staying aligned vertically. Bring arms above the head in Anjali Mudra by pressing palms together, it is commonly used in a Namaste greeting. Hold for 30 seconds then come back to Tadasana, repeat alternate side. Always breathe normally through your nose and be mindful of each move eliminating all other thoughts.

A Bowl of Tea: Respect, Purity, Tranquility, Harmony

The Japanese Tea Ceremony is called Chado and means the Way of Tea. It is the ceremonial preparation and serenity of the traditions that inform us Chado is the ceremonial quintessential spiritual experience to be repeated exactly in form and as frequently as possible to insure it takes its place as a portal to our spiritual existence.

The tea ceremony expresses the simplicity of zen and was initiated by Sen no Riyu in the early 1500s. He brought a simple totally austere method of spiritual mindfulness to the sharing of a cup of tea. Chado is held in a tearoom usually in the center of a fragrant and beautiful natural garden. The entrance to the tea room includes the Shinto practice of washing hands and mouth to purify before entering. After walking into the tearoom thru the Shoji sliding doors one is greeted by the scent of freshly picked flowers and the beauty of their presence. The entrance itself is low level so guests must bend which is a symbol of humility and everyone being equal in the way of tea as in life. The floor is constructed of tatami mats made of woven straw of about two meters. The tables are low and the guests sit on a zabutan (large pillow).

The Tea Master carries the tea bowl and whisk, scoop, napkin and tea. Tea Master has also placed the fresh water on the fire to boil in advance of the ceremony. The waste water has a container which holds the ladle and is placed in position. Each step is done according to a rigidly traditional format for the expressed purpose of a ceremonial meditation that includes respect, purity, tranquility, and harmony.

Step one — Tea Master uses a cloth and wipes the tea scoop and container indicating to all present that cleanliness exemplifies purity.

Step two — Using the ladle the tea master scoops hot water from the kettle and places it in the tea bowl with the whisk for cleaning then pours it into the waste container and wipes clean and dries everything.

Step three — The powdered tea called matcha is whipped. Tea Master ceremoniously picks up the tea in the left hand and the scoop is picked up in the right hand and three scoops of matcha is placed in the tea bowl.

Step four — The hot water is poured on the matcha and whisked and then placed in the tea masters left palm. The Tea Master then holding the tea bowl with the right hand turns it two full turns until the front of the bowl is now facing guests. The first guest picks up the bowl and holding it as the tea master did.

Step five — The guest holding the tea bowl cup turns toward the second guest and gassho back and forth. This is a "here you first… no you go first" politeness and the second guest declines.Raising the bowl in a bow to the tea master the first guest then sips tea. After savoring the tea with use of all a sentient being can use the guest respectfully concludes by cleaning the bowl with thumb and finger or a cloth of it is available.

Step six — The tea bowl can be repeated down the line or handed back to the the tea master for the process to be repeated after cleaning or handed down the line until the last guest or member of the sangha has had tea.

Step Seven — Reverse the process and clean all instruments and bowls and placing them in their appropriate place. This process is repetitive and meditative.

Drinking tea is healthy due to polyphenols which are antioxidants that neutralize free radical damage from the sun, pollution and bad diet. The most important polyphenols are catechins. The other component of tea that is most helpful is L-theanine an amino acid which produces a gradual exposure to caffeine in tea creating a more gently serene experience rather than the immediate bang of other caffeinated beverages.

Ura Senke Grand Master XV offered this message on the Chado: Served with a respectful heart and received with gratitude, a bowl of tea satisfies both physical and spiritual thirst."

APPLIED THEORY

When preparing hot tea, start with fresh water each time to insure high oxygen levels in the water. Do not use distilled water. Bring to a boil. Pour a small amount of boiling water into your cup or bowl to warm it. Place the loose-leaf tea in the French Press or the tea bag directly into the cup. White and green teas require less hot so wait a minute, black teas very hot so pour directly from the boil. Pour your water let steep oolong 7 minutes, green, 3 minutes, black tea 5 minutes. Enjoy the tea in a single tasking style, while drinking tea just drink tea. We can't repeat that single moment of today's cup of tea; "ichi-go ichi-e meaning one time, one meeting. Today's cup of tea has value, have gratitude for the experience.

GRATITUDE AND DAILY THANKS

Gratitude is a learned response that turns what we have into more than enough. A day that starts with a positive perspective, trains the mind to be happier. That includes being thankful for the people, places and things that bring joy to our lives. There will always be challenges that can promote a greater resolve toward the solution. The goal is not to allow our natural tendencies to place the negatives as prominent spotlights in our lives. We train as we might for a fitness program to achieve physical health, we practice a mindful awareness of our gratitude.

The first known use of the word gratitude was in 1523, using the Latin word gratis and Medieval Latin gratitudo meaning thankful. This informs us that gratitude is a feeling of thankfulness for what one has. It has nothing to do with what one wants. It is important to list the good stuff and then indicate appreciation to the people, places, things and spiritual or religious we thank.

Gratitude for those who have very little by American standards is learned quickly and at a younger age. There is so much to be thankful for that we will explore. The examples provided are simply what comes to mind first when hearing the words gratitude. The examples are meant to act as a catalyst in advance of starting the weekly writing that enables us to journal and then make gratitude part of our daily lives. Fear, anger, envy are not possible in our minds during concentrated thoughts of gratitude. They diminish in intensity as we practice a life of being thankful.

Gratitude enables us to embrace equanimity, which is in simple terms a more balanced life. Identifying and deconstructing our fears is vital to enjoying happier, more satisfying lives. To do this requires a systematic approach to examining questions that have been asked by philosophers since ancient times. Some of the questions we ask ourselves in this pursuit include: Why am I here on earth? How can I live a happier, calmer life? What is the meaning of my existence? How can I deal with others in a more ethical way?

Consideration of these concepts has a calming effect because it provides a plan or framework for approaching spiritual aspects of our lives apart from solely material goals. Working toward answers to these questions does not require a thorough knowledge of the history of philosophy or the various thought systems of famous philosophers. It can be achieved by the introspective journaling of exactly what we are thankful for, a gratitude diary crafted by the individual that encompasses the most significant aspects of their daily lives. It requires that one thinks about the gratitude list in a serious and mature way. Dealing with these questions makes us all philosophers.

Since the beginning of early civilization, before the written word, people have asked questions regarding the purpose of our existence and the nature of our world. Determining to what extent life has meaning is the primary task of philosophy. The questions many ask indicate our yearning to know if there is more to life than simply going through our daily routine.

We all want to find a purpose for the efforts we make beyond the pursuit of material things in an effort to improve the quality of life. Without this introspection and structure of being thankful our lives might simply be in the words of Thomas Hobbes, …solitary, poor, nasty, brutish and short. Many philosophers including historical Buddha, in different cultures and times have arrived at a similar approach to living a calmer more meaningful life.

Aristotle, one of the earliest and most significant of any of the philosophers proposed that a virtuous person lives by the principal of moderation. The principle of moderation has always guided ethical behavior. It teaches us to control our desires so they do not rule over reason. External desires are a source of unhappiness if you allow them to be. The Stoic philosophers said that you should want what you have. You will be happier wanting what you have rather than if you continually desire things.

In the words of Socrates, "The unexamined life is not worth living." Even if one thinks this is overstating the case, it has to be conceded that dealing with philosophical questions adds to the quality of our lives. Although none of us knows in advance the extent of the quality of our lives, we do have a fairly high degree of control over its quality based on our own day-to-day decisions and by exerting control over our desires. This is accomplished more quickly by examining the long list of what and who we are thankful for in our daily existence. The primary objective for each of us should be to increase the quality of our lives to the greatest extent that we can. In this way we honor our own existence and add to quality of the lives of those closest to us and about whom we care most.

The Aristotelian advice about moderation suggests personal responsibility and rational choices to create the space for balance. This in turn sets into motion the potential for progress toward the serenity of mind, body and spirit. Balance of these is essential. Equanimity is the concept that best explains this process. Equanimity is the balance of mind and soul coming from great insight. It is a skill to be learned resulting in emotional stability during stress.

Learning to stay calm during times of mental disquietude and having gratitude for what we have is the path toward equanimity. The concept of a zen existence is based on a variety of training techniques and methods in addition to the Noble Path.

The word equanimity comes from the Latin word aegis which means balanced and animus which means spirit. The ancient Greeks took it to this level and taught: Nepsis - sober observation - Ataraxia -freedom from upset - Apathis - dispassion. With equanimity we learn to fight off reactions to the limbic system's production of cortisol so stress doesn't take its ugly toll. A person becomes an observer of events free from upset and dispassionate. During personal tragedy or triumph equanimity creates balance.

As the saying goes, knowledge brings power. Introspection is a necessary step to reveal things that need to be corrected, eliminated, improved, energized or strengthened. Take an introspective journey and commit to a weekly gratitude journal. It is suggested writing once a week but feel free to write more frequently at first. The format of this suggestion is to give the reader a few starting ideas on how to keep a gratitude journal and then room to personalize it. On a daily basis begin to think of every good thing someone you met along the way has done for you or others. Feel the gratitude for those acts of kindness deep within your heart chakra. If it truly takes three weeks to create a habit solidify your commitment by more frequently writing about those acts of kindness and love with gratitude. Then progress to the suggested weekly program of I am thankful for... art, companion animals, freedom of press, electric, singing, clean water, good health, first responders, airplanes, internet, nature, music, religious freedom...

Practicing Gratitude & Equanimity:

>   decreases jealousy and envy
>   increases stress management
>   decreases anger
>   increases happiness
>   decreases fear
>   increases relationship communication
>   decreases insomnia
>   increases energy levels

An example:

I AM GRATEFUL FOR Meditation: it allows the mind to take a rest. If we are not thinking we are meditating. I am thankful for the graduate school professor who taught us the benefits of meditation and how to select one of the many meditative techniques that set the course for a more tranquil life. Taking time throughout the day to go into an opposite state of relaxation, rest and calm reminds our body that there is more than one way to be. The goal is to turn the momentum in the other direction. We attempt to turn the momentum in the other direction. Let's attempt to make calm our baseline, the norm to which our body always returns.

APPLIED THEORY

Construct a gratitude list with a minimum of 100 items. Visualize life without that list because you forgot to be grateful. Then, continue to write in a journal on a weekly basis all that you have deep gratitude for in this life.

Management of our time & A Quiet Mind

Single-Tasking

Multitasking can reduce productivity by approximately forty percent according to some researchers. Switching from one task to another makes it difficult to tune out distractions and can cause mental blocks that can slow down progress.

If you are doing several different things at once or in rapid succession you are multi-tasking. In the old days this was thought to be an excellent idea, but modern research has proven beyond any doubt that we lose valuable time when we switch between tasks thinking about it. We all know that texting impacts affects safe driving and its potential consequences. Imagine if you were operating complicated or dangerous machinery while arguing with your spouse on a cell phone.

The point here is safety, productivity and best use of your time and energy. For three-thousand years the Buddhist monks have suggested single tasking in their interpreted words of the historical Buddha: when pouring water, just pour water. When you are eating, just eat. When you are walking, just walk. Sage advice without the benefit of longitudinal studies.

It is also important to take your time when doing any task, do not rush and remember to focus on the task at hand. How many times do we hear complaints that if only we had not rushed we would have done it correctly the first time. Try to stick with the task until completed. If that is not possible because it is lunch break try staying in the mode during lunch. A single tasking lunch looks something like this: take out the bread and place it on the plate that is the first step in preparation, then remove all ingredients from the refrigerator and construct a sandwich. After eating, open the refrigerator one final time and place all the ingredients back in. Then wash down the area and wash and dry the dishes. The focus then shifts to the business task and nothing else.

Which is the more efficient way to work, single-tasking versus multitasking? According to the National Center for Biotechnology Information, at the U.S. National Library of Medicine, the average attention span of a human being has decreased from 12 seconds in the year 2000 to 8 seconds in the year 2013. This next fact will blow your mind. The attention span of the average goldfish is 9 seconds. Yes, what you are thinking is correct. Our attention span is one-second shorter than that of a common goldfish. What has caused a 4 second decrease in our attention span over the past 14 or so years? The answer might be the over stimulation we receive from the internet, smartphones and other media outlets. We constantly have our faces in our phones, computers, or tablets checking social media, national and local news, sports, stocks, our electronic planner for the day, miscellaneous articles and entertaining videos.

We are constantly being bombarded with information from every direction, so naturally we all morph into multi-taskers. We will have seven tabs open on our desktop while simultaneously talking on the phone while sending an email and fumbling through our papers on our desk. It is believed that multitasking is the most efficient way to work. You get more accomplished in a shorter period of time. But is multitasking really more efficient? Is the quality of work as up to snuff if you would have devoted all your time and attention to one single task? The answer is no. Multitasking is not an efficient way to work. In the case of multitasking, more is less.

In September 2014, a study was published by researchers at the University of Sussex that came to the conclusion that smartphone and other media devices may be changing human brain structure. An excerpt from the published study:

"Individuals who engaged in more media multitasking activity had smaller gray matter volumes in the anterior cingulate cortex. This could also possibly explain the poorer cognitive control performance and negative socio-emotional outcomes associated with increased media-multitasking. While the cross-sectional nature of our study does not allow us to specify the direction of causality, our results brought to light novel associations between individual media multitasking behaviors and anterior cingulate cortex structure differences."

Kep Kee Loh, Ryota Kanai. *Higher Media Multi-Tasking Activity Is Associated with Smaller Gray-Matter Density in the Anterior Cingulate Cortex. PLoS ONE, 2014; 9 (9): e106698 DOI: 10.1371/journal.pone.0106698*

Multitasking leads to a lack of efficiency. Have you ever been in a meeting while trying to respond to emails or text messages at the same time? You are trying to listen to the speaker at a meeting and trying to respond effectively to a client or co-worker on your phone. While doing all of this you are half listening to the speaker, and because you are half listening, you are distracted and send the wrong email or text to the wrong client. By the end of the meeting you have missed the majority of what the meeting was actually about. On top of that, you have confused and had to explain yourself to multiple clients or coworkers. Now imagine if you had single-tasked and devoted your full attention first and foremost to the meeting. Then after the meeting you gave your full attention and focus to the client/coworker issue. You would have paid attention in the meeting and been well informed and involved. You may have even given an insightful thought or idea and impressed a manager showing your attentiveness. The client or co-worker issue would have been solved in one concise text message or email with zero confusion and zero added stress in probably less time.

In a study done at the Institute of Psychiatry by University of London psychologist Dr. Glenn Wilson showed that those who attempted to multitask, such as talking on the phone while simultaneously returning emails, saw a 10 point fall in their IQ. This has an equivalent effect on the mind as going a night without sleep. Researchers suggested that this is double the amount of points dropped compared to studies done on the impact of smoking marijuana.

While attempting to complete multiple tasks at once we trick ourselves into thinking that we are getting more done, when in actuality the opposite is true. We are getting less done. According to a study done by Neuroscientist Earl Miller, when the human brain is presented with multiple visual stimulants, only one or two stimulants activate the brain. This shows that our brain can only focus on one or two different things at a time. When we try to multitask we overload our brain. Tasks that tend to be similar in nature struggle to use the same portion of the brain for computation. An example used earlier was talking on the phone while responding to emails. Because of this competition for attention between the tasks our brain function becomes slower. This causes your mind to jump between tasks which slows down your productivity compared to if you focus solely on a single task until its completion.

Multitasking can also have a negative impact on your health. When attempting to complete multiple tasks your mind jumps from one task to another. This constant interruption hinders your productivity. This slowed productivity means that it is actually taking longer for tasks to get done. This lack of productivity can lead to frustration and stress. You become overwhelmed when you feel you are juggling too many tasks. When your stress level increases your body releases adrenaline and cortisol, the stress hormones. Adrenaline increases your heart rate and raises blood pressure. Cortisol increases sugars in the form of glucose in the bloodstream. Long term exposure to cortisol can put you at risk for anxiety, depression, weight gain, and heart disease, not to mention it can damage the region of the brain that deals with memory.

Single-tasking means just that. Focusing on one task at a time allows you to put your mind into just that task. You limit distractions and interruptions until completion. This allows all of your brain power to be applied. This will make sure that the task is completed the most efficient way possible to the best of your ability without the added stress or interruption. Your level of productivity, quality of the work done, and information retention will all increase by single-tasking.

To break the multitasking habit and switch to single-tasking will be difficult at first. It will seem that your time is not being utilized to its full potential. Remember the facts previously presented and remind yourself that you are putting out a better quality of work and are reducing stress levels.

The first step in making the switch from multitasking to single tasking is being conscious and catching yourself when you are multitasking. Be aware and then re-focus on the single task at hand. To help limit distractions and interruptions start by cleaning up your workspace. Clean the clutter from your desk and create an organized clean area to work. A clutter free room is a clutter free mind. Log out of social media to limit distractions. Turn your cellphone off or limit the use to family emergencies only while focusing on the task at hand. If important things come up while you are single-tasking, write them down on a notebook or sticky note, and continue until your task is finished. Limit the number of tabs open on your browser to two at the most, preferably one tab.

In order to single-task properly one needs to learn how to prioritize. This starts with making a list of what needs to get done and looking at the importance and urgency of the tasks.

Focusing on one task at a time allows you to put your mind into just that task. This will make sure that the task is completed the most efficient way possible to the best of your ability without the added stress or interruption.

When pouring water just pour water.

I am so busy are the four words we hear daily from friends, family and coworkers. Are we all really so very busy or is it now a virtue to appear as if we are? It is interesting that the feeling of faster and busier is the norm and equates with feeling more productive. We seem to be informing everyone constantly just how busy we are these days. It is time to fine tune our thinking on why we are so busy and if we are as productive as we can be. Even the use of costly electronic planning systems can fail to keep us on schedule if we don't get to the root cause of our constant running in circles.

Let's begin. Write down everything that you do from the minute you get up in the morning until the minute you shut your eyes. Everything! Write down or photo journal all activities including brushing your teeth, twenty-minute showers, an extra hour on social media, day dreaming, chat time at the water cooler in the office, delayed pick-ups at the distributor, flirting with the new office manager absolutely everything. A comparison can then be made to the way things will change after implementing the ideas in this book.

Introspection is a necessary step. It reveals things that may need to be corrected, eliminated, improved, energized or strengthened.

Building a balanced life begins with eliminating stressful actions and cultivating good ones. There is no reason to wait. Choose to begin the lifelong process of cultivating and cherishing your well-being and make the commitment immediately.

The intention of these pages is to provide an easy to follow template with the objective of working towards physical, emotional and spiritual wellness. While the following chapters are full of techniques that you can use to improve the quality of your life over the long term, what you will find below are five suggestions that will, if put into practice right now, produce an immediate difference in your day-to-day life. The common thread between them is simplicity and spirituality. The shelves of bookstores are filled from wall-to-wall with overcomplicated solutions to the issues we will confront in the following pages. It may be over-complication that prevents progress.

In the 14th Century, English theologian William of Occam reasoned that "It is vain to do with more what can be done by fewer." Several centuries later, those words are still extremely significant.

If so desired, this very moment can be the beginning of a new era in your life. Ignore poor choices you have made in the past – yesterday exists only in your mind – and embrace the here and now. The only reality is the one we exist in right at this very moment. Live in the moment, and make informed choices that will make every subsequent moment a step in the direction of your personal spiritual goals. This type of attitude will make both the journey and the destination more rewarding.

You owe it to yourself to take proper care of your mind, body and spirit. In just a short period of time each day, it is possible to dramatically alter the course of your life in an exceptionally positive direction. Be honest with yourself.

Admitting that you're fearful of something is nothing to be ashamed of. Fear is often unfairly viewed as weakness, but by applying an approach of non-judgmental self-awareness, you can identify your fears and anxieties, formulate a plan that addresses specifically how you can deconstruct them and reclaim the energy they steal from you.

Be specific. Identify exactly what creates your procrastination. For example, if money or lack thereof is a problem, break down exactly what is happening with your income and spending. Are you spending on credit, purchasing luxury items you don't need? Are you spending it to impress superficial people that don't deserve your attention? Are you paying higher interest rates on your credit cards because you procrastinated paying a bill and went into universal default enabling the creditors to increase the interest rates?

Set goals. One's ambitions are very unique to the individual. Therefore, for our purposes we will define attainment of a goal by the position of where you currently find yourself in life, relative to where you would like to be. Setting attainable objectives is essential to making steady progress. When goals are set in a systematic fashion, adjusted according to results, and followed reliably, there is a much increased chance of an individual achieving success in his or her chosen endeavor.

Though goal-setting is easier when the objective is tangible, progress can still be observed in ventures where the destination is not as clear-cut. For example, if the macro goal is "omit procrastination," that particular classification is much too broad. It must be dissected into more manageable parts. The sources of procrastination can be analyzed rationally and identified. Once that happens, steps should be taken to eliminate the causes. If it is not possible to eliminate them – and of course, it often isn't – a practice of management takes place. Be assured that however daunting the task may seem, it is possible to overcome even the most distressing situations and occurrences.

Recognize your needs. You are an individual. As such, you have very specific needs. Pay attention to them. While it may seem obvious that an individual should be acutely aware of his or her own needs, it is easily forgotten amidst the steady torrent of unsolicited bad advice that is received throughout the day from assorted co-workers, fair-weather friends, casual acquaintances, and even family members.

Realize that no one knows what is better for you than you do. Accordingly, you should look deep inside yourself and form an opinion about what is necessary to make your life better. When you have arrived at a sensible conclusion, arrive at a series of realistic ambitions.

Set your intention. Whether the proposed remedy includes use of a monthly planner, twenty-five minutes of meditation per night, a healthier diet, regular fitness practice, or a combination of each, form a plan and implement it. It may be helpful to write it down so you can refer back to it later. This will help you assess progress.

It is the case with most long-term endeavors that staying on track is often the most difficult aspect. Simple solutions to common problems are presented, with attention to both short-term and long-term time management. If you are not sure about one of the techniques suggested in the book, approach it with a degree of skepticism without outright cynicism. Try the discipline in question for a few weeks and see how it affects you.

While it is worthwhile to master dozens of time management strategies, maybe you'll experience your best results with just four or five, used a few times per week.

Find what works. Your results will be highly individual and may require a certain degree of experimentation before you will arrive at the desired level of success. With persistence, short-term goals will adapt into long-term accomplishments. For example, at the time you first read this, maybe you're only able to meditate for two minutes or so before your mind starts to wander. Be patient. At first, set your meditation timer for five minutes. A week later, set it for ten. Eventually, you'll work your way up to twenty-five minutes. The use of a variety of time management techniques will enhance your ability to avoid procrastination, set priorities and plan.

Stick to the plan. Avoid frustration by taking note of the incremental progress you make. If it takes you three months to achieve a properly executed monthly planning session, it will give you an even greater sense of accomplishment than if you are able to do it on your first try.

If it takes one year of steady progression to acquire tools that will serve you for a lifetime, that is a winning proposition. Conversely, it may not take a year, or even a month to see progress.

Make your success work for you, not against you. Irrespective of the period of time that it takes you to advance, enjoy the process and enjoy your progress.

Motivate yourself. Motivation means different things to different people. It comes from many sources – from within, from the support of others, from ideas and actions. What is always constant however, is that the will of a person to allow his or her self to become motivated when the stimulus necessitates it. Before each change, sit down quietly and focus on the value you hope to gain.

Overcome obstacles. The goal is to put you in control of properly handling the inevitable challenges that life is full of; doing so with attention not only towards maintaining and surviving rigorous schedules, but advancing and progressing in the midst of it. If you feel like you are getting sidetracked, review your goals. Be patient, consistent and stay in the present. If you can adhere to these simple guidelines, you will find yourself always moving forward and taking pride in your accomplishments.

APPLIED THEORY

- Affirm concepts that are essential, yet often forgotten or ignored.
- Relax and refocus.
- Appreciate what you have instead of dwelling on what you don't.
- Remember that change is inevitable.
- Break with old patterns that hold you back from your potential.
- Prevent negative thoughts and negative people from controlling your life.
- Embrace optimism.

MEDIATION AND MINDFULNESS

Silencing the mind by meditative concentration is increased by the silence creating the inner peace that opens the door to one-pointed meditation. While meditating we target something for the mind to concentrate on, which will give tranquility. The targeted effects of reciting a mantra, watching a candle burn, visualizing a cresting wave over and over again, or simply concentrating on breathing creates the environment for serene meditation from consciousness to super consciousness. One should start with ten minutes a day, and progress to twenty.

Meditation is usually performed regularly in the morning and evening. It may be performed alone, or in a group. It involves sitting in silence with the back straight and centered, keeping the body still, taking deep breaths, and keeping the mind still. Seated meditation is a practice of sitting in stillness that ultimately allows us to experience a higher awareness. During the day's activities, try to remind yourself to keep proper posture with the back, similar to the posture taken when meditating. This helps keep focus on the activity at hand, and the effort of engaging in good posture helps quiet the mind during a stressful day.

The calming effects of meditation can impact you positively both mentally and physically by reducing stress, increasing energy and enhancing mental clarity. Meditation focuses the mind's attention on a certain thought or feeling. Accordingly, when meditating, focus on what you want, not on what you don't. Keep an inward mental focus. Focus allows the mind to concentrate without interference from other outside thoughts. Looking inward can help improve your connection with the external world. Visualization focuses the mind's attention on an act or movement, making a connection between the imagination and subconscious.

Mindfulness is a mental state achieved by focusing one's awareness on the present moment, while calmly acknowledging and accepting one's feelings, thoughts, and bodily sensations, used as a therapeutic technique.

How to Meditate:

Find a quiet place.

Eliminate distractions such as cell phones, television, and computers.

Get comfortable.

Choose a comfortable position, preferably one of the following:
* Upright on a chair
* On a cushion
* Cross-legged
* Lotus or Half-Lotus posture
* Burmese seated position
* Kneeling, with the posterior on a bench or supported by a cushion

Keep a straight back.

The Mala Beads are used to assist in mantra meditation, they normally have 108 beads with one special being called the Guru bead. The Mala beads are used in conjunction with the breath and mantra alternating to help maintain equanimity during the meditation. The use of the Mala beads includes an understanding that the index finger is never used nor does it even touch the beads. This is a reminder that the index finger represents the ego and Buddhism is egoless.

The use of the Mala beads follows a specific, essentially standard practice. Holding the Mala in your right hand between the thumb and all of the fingers except the index finger that simply points out. Once secure and in position start with the Guru Bead and draw the beads toward you.

Pull each bead toward you and on pulling the thumb forward inhale pull back then exhale. Mantra can be your own or you can use Om.

When you reach the Guru bead again never cross over it. When you reach the Guru bead gently twist your right wrist toward your body extending your thumb under the Guru bead then slip the middle fingers under the beads. You are now moving in the opposite direction but did not pass over the Guru bead.

Focus your attention on breathing or a Mantra. A mantra can be a poem, prayer, phrase, chant or word such as OM.

Center breathing on the Hara line which is the line that runs vertically up the center of the body.

If the mind wanders, bring it back to your breath or mantra. Focus on positive thoughts and/or visualize a tranquil setting.

It may be helpful to set a timer if so desired when it is time for you to re-enter full consciousness.

Kinhin A Walking Meditation:

Labyrinths are ancient human symbols known to go back at least 3,500 years. They appeared on most inhabited continents in prehistory, with examples known from North & South America, Africa, Asia and across Europe from the Mediterranean to Scandinavia. The labyrinth symbol was incorporated into the floors of the great Gothic pilgrimage cathedrals of France in the twelfth & thirteenth centuries. An example of a famous design is the nave of the Cathedral of Notre Dame de Chartres outside of Paris. This labyrinth was built of honey-colored limestone with marble lines around the year 1200.

Walking in a labyrinth is walking meditation. The use of intuition when walking the path is a right brain task. If a person elects to enter, they are clearly making a choice toward a spiritual path that is represented by the labyrinth structure. It might be said that walking into the labyrinth is a metaphor for walking toward your core. Labyrinths are described as being "unicursal" – when you walk in and around the way out is the exact same way in. It is not a maze or puzzle to be solved; a labyrinth is a path in and out.

Research conducted at the Harvard Medical School's Mind/Body Medical Institute by Dr. Herbert Benson has found that focused walking meditations are highly efficient at reducing anxiety and eliciting what Dr. Benson calls the 'relaxation response'. This effect has significant long-term health benefits, including lower blood pressure and breathing rates, reduced incidents of chronic pain, reduction of insomnia, improved fertility, and many other benefits. Regular meditative practice leads to greater powers of concentration and a sense of control and efficiency in one's life. Labyrinth walking is among the simplest forms of focused walking meditation.

Guidelines For Walking A Labyrinth:

- Pause at the entrance to center yourself
- Keep your mind receptive
- Walk with purpose and focus
- Pause at the center to open your mind to new insights
- After exiting the Labyrinth, reflect quietly on your experience

Taking Care of Yourself

Preventive changes can affect the quality and quantity of life if Implemented and maintained. There is a preponderance of evidence indicating that we can do more by preventing and staying away from dangerous or risky behaviors than treating after the fact. Prophylaxis is a Greek word meaning to guard or prevent beforehand. This book explores the journey of mind, body and spirit balance.

There is no doubt that many of us experience stress throughout the day in both our personal and professional lives. Sometimes we do not even realize how tense we are until we set aside a moment to sit down and take a personal inventory of how we are feeling.

Do you have a mind racing with thoughts and constant lists of tasks that need to be accomplished? Do you notice areas of your body that are constantly tense? Are you living in a Perpetual state of stress? Stress can have a variety of harmful effects on the body and mind from depression, anxiety, sleep disorders, headaches, ulcers and some even suggest cancer. It is well documented that stress has a profound impact on the health of the body and mind. As an example, let's take a look at the number one killer in the United States for both men and women: heart disease.

It is time to claim back our lives and bring ourselves into harmony with a natural state of healing and well-being that can be accessed by anyone. A mind and body that is constantly bombarded with stress signals a stimulation of the sympathetic nervous system which never has time to recover. Eventually, it is as if we become carried away by the momentum of stress, and we forget how to be any other way. Taking time throughout the day to go into an opposite state of relaxation, rest, calm and happiness reminds our body that there is more than one way to be. The goal is to turn the momentum in the other direction. Let's attempt to make calm our baseline, the norm to which our body always returns. Challenging situations will always arise and stress in certain situations can be a healthy way to keep us focused on handling a problem or accomplishing a task.

However, once the challenge is over, many bodies fail to return to a restful state because we are so accustomed to stress and anxiety. In order to accomplish this baseline of tranquility, we must immerse ourselves in activities that bring about this state of rest.

One technique that has proven to be especially effective in the area of stress reduction is meditation through guided visualizations. Meditation has become a very popular buzz word in the United States as people search desperately for ways to bring their lives back into balance and mitigate the effects of stress on their minds, bodies and spirits. Some forms of meditation instruct practitioners to bring single pointed focus to their breath or to a mantra, a short phrase that is repeated over and over. It can be difficult to sustain this type of practice because our minds have become accustom to racing with a variety of thoughts and our bodies are programed for productivity.

While mindfulness and mantra meditation, if practiced consistently throughout one's life, can certainly bring about calm and insight, many end up abandoning the practice before they are able to realize any of the potential benefits. One reason for this may be that it is simply a difficult way to accomplish the goal of mastering tranquility. An alternative of guided imagery is not very different from mantra meditation, in a sense.

The purpose of mantras is to keep the mind focused and to perhaps guide the practitioner towards transcendental states through forgetting oneself and breaking past the boundaries of the ego-mind. Why does a mantra necessarily have to be one phrase? Could a mantra not be an entire guided visualization meditation? This would serve a similar purpose. Guided visualizations bring the mind into single pointed concentration, allowing distractions of a racing mind to drop away. In fact, guided visualizations can be even more effective in achieving this end because it engages the mind, body and spirit in an all-inclusive journey. Guided imagery calls all of the senses together by leading one into a scenario where sight, sound, smell, touch, action, feeling and emotion are activated. Engaging the entire body enhances the ability to sustain a concentrated state. This brings us to the topic at hand of guided visualization. Scientists explain that mental images activate processes in the body in a nearly identical way as actually perceiving the objects in reality. Mental imagery engages certain areas of the brain and then has an effect on the nervous systems. Emotional centers of the brain, particularly the amygdala, will respond. This area is known to play a role in emotions such as anger and fear. There has been much research on the effects of viewing or imagining threatening images. The body will actually respond with an increase in heart rate and respirations. (Kosslyn, Ganis & Thompson, 2001).

Guided imagery has been known to activate the parasympathetic nervous system creating a range of beneficial responses such as reduced anxiety, lowered heart rate and blood pressure, relaxation of blood vessels, slower breathing rate and increased digestion and absorption of food.

Guided Visualizations:

Majestic View of the Snow-Capped Mountain

Prepare for a meditative journey high above the Blue Ridge Mountains where the lenticular clouds hover like a massive dome over the Kittatinny range.

Calm your body and refocus your mind lie face up with your hands and legs relaxed and your head and neck on a pillow.

Focus on your breath, only the breath let thoughts go. Inhale, exhale...inhale, exhale....inhale, exhale....inhale and hold it.

Now exhale.

Your body is releasing tension. Feel your jaw relax and your shoulders sink down into the mat, your legs feel as if you are floating. Inhale cool air and fill your body. Exhale the tense hot air you have been holding. Your body is totally relaxed.

Replace negative thoughts with positive affirmations. Set your intention to climb up and out of your stressful existence.

Visualize yourself floating on a soft white cumulous cloud.

It is cotton like and puffy and looks like cauliflower. It is the fair weather cloud and a nice place to be. Living our lives in calmness and fair weather. Visualizing the serenity of equanimity and loving kindness. Hold on to your cloud and be safe, protected from all the ups and downs that the pressures of life toss at us.

Hold on and experience the tranquility of your ride as a place you want to be in this lifetime.

You are rising up now as your cloud moves higher relaxed and resting with your arms and legs stretched out and floating.

Look at the panoramic view of the mountain range. Looking up to see the nimbus and cirrus clouds. The gray covering that appears to be curling locks of hair almost in ringlets is misting with a slight drizzle.

As in life when we are faced with the fog we hold tight to our fair weather cloud and move forward. Now in view the rain snow sleet and hail from a dark nimbus high about the horizon but it passes quickly if we maintain the evenness of equanimity. We visualize ourselves holding our place on the fair weather cloud and break through the storms to the majestic view of the snow-capped mountain range. Open your heart and eyes to nature's beauty.

Enjoy the ride with gratitude for the ability to see and feel and smell the wondrous sights of a magnificent mountain range.

Gratitude for what we do have. Gratitude for our good health and love of family and friends.

Ride down now on your tranquil cloud to the bottom of the mountain to a calming visual of resting near a beautiful stream that is filled by the snow running off the mountain. Feel the safety of the ground beneath you and knowing you are firmly grounded to earth"s magnetic core. Grounded, in survival skills that serve you in life in the day to day trials and tribulations. Grounded in your ability to maintain balance in the face of any adversity.

Begin to slowly stretch as you sit up to take a last look at the serene stream flowing gently past your feet. Move your fingers and wiggle your toes. Open your eyes and breathe deeply.

From the seated position rise slowly and stand tall.

Raise your hands up toward the mountain toward the sky
and say 'I am grateful for my good health and love of family
and friends'

d'ecclesis

Snowing Like A Russian Novel

It's snowing like a Russian novel with freezing temperatures, but you move forward because today is the day you will Nordic ski.

Feel the wind and ice forming on your face and every area of exposed skin. Walk slowly toward the paths available in the clearing.

North will take you down a trail of prepared pites or parallel groves cut in the snow. It is neatly cut by machines and frequently the choice of the cross-country skier.

South heads out into a mountain of snow untouched by anything except nature. The choice is obvious. With the full realization that opening a track through deep snow can be arduous you move forward, placing your snow boots into the ski and picking up your poles.

The basket at the end of each pole assures you that you won't sink too deeply into the beautiful white powder.

The poles pushing off of the classic ski motion, left leg push right pole, right leg push left pole. Rhythmic, repetitive motion gliding with each stride releasing endorphins and keeping you in the now.

The poles for steadiness and propulsion feel like extensions of your arms and move with you as extended limbs.

Rhythmic, pulsating, gliding forward on flat terrain up and down small hills without breaking the stride of this walking meditation. Left, right, left, right there is no thinking now only the beautiful cadence of the rhythm. If you are thinking you are not meditating.

Feel the pulse of the motion and the joy of being out in the natural beauty of the winter forest.

See your breath as you exhale in the cold crisp air, and feel the rhythm of your breathing in sync with the movement of the skis.

You are alone and at peace with your solitude. The isolation and lack of communication is growing on you as you leave the sounds of the city behind. They are exchanged with sounds of winter birds chirping, little red foxes looking out from behind their hutches and magnificent bucks with brown shaggy fur snorting like ponies.

The smells of the forest are overwhelming with the heightened senses in this environment. All of the cabins have cedar aroma from burning logs in their fireplaces.

Breathe in the beauty and breathe out the stressors. There is a familiar smell of family and fun and a spiritual awakening from the pine forest, bringing up memories of joyful Christmas aromas.

Breathe in the joyful scents and breathe out the mental disquietude.

Stop for a rest and sip nourishment from your water bottle. Replenish your cells with the fluid of life. Value the moment and allow yourself to be happy. Relish the moment as feeling really alive with gratitude for who you are and what you have.

Prepare to climb the hill in front of you as there will always be hills and valleys in life. Spreading your skis out so they look like the letter V, herringbone up the hill with a passion to reach the other side, feeling a sense of accomplishment as your reach the crest.

Take a deep breath, hold it... counting down from five.

Push off to glide down the hill at a faster speed pointing your skis inward to snowplow and control your descent.

Acceptance that change is inevitable for the rest of this ride because at the bottom is a frozen lake. Hitting the lake at full speed in the skating motion of the cross-country skier allows you to change on a dime as is often the case with the trials and tribulations of life.

Pushing first with the right leg as an ice skater and shifting all of your weight to the right leg you find your cadence once again and soon settle in with a feeling of balance and grace gliding through life and across the large lake to the other side.

Transfer your weight to control the glide and slide into the snow completing the journey with a feeling of success, a joyful job well done and the serenity of the meditation known as mastering tranquility.

d'ecclesis

APPLIED THEORY

Concentration exercises enhance mindfulness. Select a paragraph from a book and count the words but do it without touching the printed word or pointing your finger. Next, draw a cube and color part of it but when you look at it try to see the cube not the colored area. Finally, pick up an apple and look at it, nothing else having no thoughts staying very calm giving it your undivided attention, simply observe and clear your mind. breathing in breathing out...

SHINTOISM AS A SPIRITUAL PRACTICE

Shinto, or Shintoism, is one of the oldest religions of Japan and uniquely Japanese. It teaches that Japan is the country of the Gods and people there are descendants. Shintoism is unique in that it is an action-centered religion with high importance placed on ritual practices that are carried out thoroughly to create a deep spiritual connection between the present and the ancients of the past. There are no specific guidelines or a "code of ethics" like many other religions contain as in "this is good, this is bad. Do this, do not do that". Shinto teaches important ethical principles but has no commandments.

The name Shinto is derived from the Chinese characters for Shen meaning "divine being" and Tao meaning "way". Therefore, Shinto means "way of the spirits" or "way of the Gods". What also makes Shintoism unique is that it originated and is practiced strictly in Japan and Japan only. Shintoism is deeply rooted and values the traditions and history of Japan. What makes it nearly impossible to practice Shintoism elsewhere is the importance placed on shrines. Shrines hold a deep importance and are the backbone of the religion. There are between 80,000 and 100,000 Shinto shrines spread throughout Japan. There are a few in the United States. The process of studying the traditions of Shinto as one of the most extraordinary religions provides impetus to travel to and learn from the ancient religion.

Shintoism has no specific God and there is no founder of the religion. There is not a specific scripture such as the Bible for Christians or Qur'an for Islam. Many experts cannot even agree on the time period that Shinto may have begun. At the heart of Shinto is the devotion to spiritual beings and powers which are referred to as kami which exist in nature. Shintoism is very nature driven. Kami can be defined in English as "spirit", "spiritual essence", or "God". The divine or sacred essence can manifest in many forms such as a tree, rock, body of water, animal, a place, or even a person. Those practicing Shinto believe that people and kami exist in the same world and are interconnected. A focus of Shinto is to honor one's family kami and ancestors.

The religion of Shintoism has been broken down into categories. There are many different sects and schools, but most scholars can agree on the three main categories of Shinto, the first being Shrine Shinto. This category focuses strongly in worshiping local shrines kept in the home and also taking part in events held at local shrines around one's living area. Another type of Shinto is Folk Shinto. The focus of this category is the numerous folk beliefs in spirits and gods although many of the beliefs seem to be uneven and disjointed. Followers of Folk Shinto tend to believe in spirit possession and healing from the source of a shaman. The beliefs and practices of Folk Shinto come from local ancient traditions which are why the beliefs are so fragmented. However, some practices are influenced by Buddhism, Taoism or Confucianism.

The third category is Sect Shinto. Sect Shinto was created in the 1890s with the purpose to separate government owned shrines from local organized religious communities. The difference between Shrine Shinto and Sect Shinto is that the followers of Sect Shinto believe that through the power of their consciousness they can identify a founder of Shinto, a set of teachings, and sacred scriptures.

Again, no matter what category of Shinto a person falls under there is still a heavy importance placed on shrines. Shrines are where a person worships a kami or spirit. Public shrines are sacred places that act as an access point to a kami. People visit them to pray or make offerings of food. Shrines can be man-made or pure natural places such as a tree, waterfall, or a mountain. Shrines that are natural are referred to as mori.

Many public shrines are elaborate structures whose architecture will fit the period in which the shrine was built with appropriate traditional Japanese design. At the entrance to these shrines is a Japanese gate called a tori. The tori is made of two uprights and two crossbars. The purpose of the tori is to show a division between the common world and a sacred area. At most shrines there will only be one way of access, but some shrines will have two ways of access and both paths will have a tori. Although all tori contain two uprights and two crossbars there are around twenty styles based on the kami being worshiped and the lineage of the local area and shrine. At these shrines it is common to see other barriers that act as separations from the common world and the sacred spiritual world and shrine grounds. There are clear barriers like fences, ropes, gated paths, and statues of protection.

The practice of visiting a shrine is called Omairi. It is important to note that one does not have to identify as Shinto in order to visit a shrine.

There are steps to take when visiting a shrine and the steps can vary depending on the shrine, season, holiday, or overall reason for the visit depending on what a person is praying or making an offering for. At any entrance to the shrine one should bow respectfully before passing through the tori. Typically there is a hand washing basin provided near the shrine. There is a specific way in which to cleanse one's hands. Hold the ladle in the right hand and scoop up water and pour it onto the left hand. Then transfer the ladle to the left hand and pour water onto the right hand. Place the ladle in the right hand again, make a cup with the left hand, and pour water into the left hand. Take the water from the left hand and sip it into the mouth. Quietly swish the water around in the mouth then spit the water back into the cupped left hand. After, grab the ladle handle with both hands and turn it vertically so the remaining water washes over the handle. Place the ladle where it was found.

After a proper hand cleansing is completed one can approach the shrine. Some shrines may have a bell and this would be the appropriate time to ring the bell. Other shrines may have a donation box to deposit a donation in before ringing the bell. It is appropriate and expected to leave a donation based on the level or impact of one's prayer. After donating or ringing the bell, or both, bow twice, clap twice holding the second clap. One should hold their hands together in front of the heart for a closing bow after a prayer is made.

One should be as quiet as possible while on the sacred grounds and at the shrine. No shoes should be worn in any buildings on the sacred grounds. One must be respectful and sincere to all staff and others visiting the shrine. Pay attention to areas where people are not permitted to go on the shrine grounds.

Shinto 7 ~ 5 ~ 3

The Shinto Seven~Five~Three Festival is celebrated on November 15 to show gratitude that children of this ages have healthy and happy lives. On that date several parents approach the local Shinto Shrine with three-year-old children dressed in red if they are female and grey if male. The older girls wear the obi sash for the first time in public. Various sets of parents begin to explain the traditions after they take their first bow at the entrance. The parents and elders explain the importance of nature, the ritual purification and cleanliness and the worship of the Kami spirits.

Shinto explains that 3, 5, 7 are considered to be lucky numbers in Japan and perhaps that also explains why it is on the 15th as the numbers add up to 15! The Shinto Priests promoted trained and ordained are suggested by members of the community. The Priests wave a branch high above the heads of the children calling in the Kami and praying for continued good health for all children. All children in Japan are registered ethnic Shinto in their towns and communities at birth by the local Shrines. At that time they are taken to the Shrine as infants and receive a guardian bag. The little ones carry that bag as they now return for the festival called Chichi-Go-San. All children enjoy the pink candy given at festival called "Thousand Year" and many tiny toy dogs are also given by family and friends as gifts. The children are taught to write notes and pray to the Kami spirits for healthy and prosperous lives.

There is a tiny three-year-old girl in her beautiful red kimono and hair done like mommy. She sits near an empty seat and appears to be having a conversation with an imaginary friend. The child insists she is talking to a Kami who joined the 7-5-3 festival which apparently only she can see. She asks the Kami for more toys and candy and good health not only for herself but all people of Japan especially her parents and family. Hearing this from the little one the parents and both sets of grandparents jump up from their seats and almost in unison deep bow to the empty seat the smallest child believes is occupied by her personal Kami friend and protector. Respect, reverence and ritual cohesively form the essence of Shintoism.

The spirituality of Shinto teaches the unity of nature:
>Tradition and the family
>Love of nature
>Physical cleanliness
>Worship ancestral spirits

>>*Tall American*
>>*Bows Prays Kami Ancestors*
>>*Ducks Through Temple Gate*
>>*d'ecclesis*

APPLIED THEORY

Set up an altar of your choice. Use the Omairi steps to prepare. Bow respectfully before passing into the altar/shrine area. Hand washing traditionally occurs holding the ladle in the right hand, which scoops up water, pouring it into the left hand. Then transfer the ladle to the left hand and pour water onto the right hand. Make a cup with the left hand and pour water in, sipping it into the mouth. Swish the water before spitting it out. Bow twice, clap twice, gassho. Write a note with your wish or intention and place it in a spiritual bowl on your altar.

Saint Ignatius Loyola's 'Spiritual Exercises'

Early in the 16th Century a Spanish priest named Saint Ignatius of Loyola created a spiritual system of exercises to enhance individual participation in establishing transformative spirituality. The meditations were suggested to be taught by a spiritual mentor or theologian over a period of several weeks in a retreat setting. All were invited to participate, including lay people. Saint Ignatius later became the founder of Society of Jesus, or Jesuits. Spiritual exercises required silence and solitude, but discernment is at the core of the exercises, the choice of ethical thought in making the correct choices between right and wrong.

While practicing the spiritual exercises in the retreat setting of solitude Ignatius wrote that we should question in a classic contemplative way some questions which he calls "application of the senses."

* *{Louis J. Puhl, SJ Translation - The "Spiritual Exercises" Ignation Spirituality 7 MARCH. 2017 :121-126.}*

Saint Ignatius suggested we should *"Place yourself in a scene from the Gospels… Ask yourself, 'What do I see? What do I hear? What do I feel, taste and smell?'* *

Father *James Martin: An Introduction to Ignatian contemplation American Magazine. 21 September. 2016.*

In the second exercise Loyola says: *"I will call to memory all the sins of my life, looking at them year by year or period by period. For these three things will be helpful: first, the locality of house where I lived; second, the associations which I had with others; third, the occupation I was pursuing. I will ponder looking at the foulness and evil if it were not forbidden."*

Spiritual Exercises are a traditional and classic way to delve into a more spiritual life as a Christian. They were from the year 1545! There are thousands of spiritual retreats run around the world asking many of the same questions as to how can I transform into a more spiritual life in the case Saint Ignatius both spiritual and religious. Loyola was the primary source for these ideas and the implementation of the program.

On the subject of eating: *"While one is eating one can use a different consideration, drawn from a life of some pious contemplation, or some spiritual project at hand. When the attention is thus directed to some good object, a person will be less concerned with the sensible pleasure from the bodily food. Above all, one should be on guard against being totally absorbed in what one is eating or letting oneself be completely dominated by the appetite. Rather, one should be master of oneself, both in the manner of eating and the amount one takes."*

The most significant exercise is planning for the next day and meal: *"To rid oneself of disordered excess it is very profitable, after dinner or supper or at some other hour when the appetite to eat or drink in not strong, to settle with ones self how much food is to be taken at the next dinner or supper. Then, one should not exceed this amount either because of appetite and of temptation of disordered appetite."* With all the fad diets today, Saint Loyola nearly five-hundred years ago presented one that really does work.

Who was Ignatius? He was born in Spain and lost his mother shortly after birth, so he was raised by the help of his family. As a teen he joined the army for to see the world and serve his country. During battle his legs were hit by a cannonball and he was returned to his father's home for treatment and recuperation. While receiving the medical care of the day he began to read for the first time in his life and a spiritual conversion was in its early stages. Ignatius elected to study more of his religion and elected to read about mediations called simple contemplations that suggested visualization of Gospel stories such as placing oneself at the Nativity. Thus his transformation from vain glorious soldier to spiritual guide began.

He learned the process of discernment and values of using the heart and mind to make better choices. The Christian concepts of good versus evil and God's will were also examined. Ignatius joined the Benedictine monastery of Sunta Maria in Monserrat to examine his past transgressions and lifestyle. He was as a youngster a ladies man and liked to party. This introspection led to what many before him have done as they become more self-actualized and spiritual. Ignatious gave up his expensive clothes to the poor, and his accumulated wealth and dramatically placed his sword at the Virgin's altar. Ignatious went into a long period of solitude praying in a cave in the grotto and practiced asceticism. He lived as a beggar, ate and drank sparingly and wore a sackcloth. Loyola's spiritual awakening on the banks of the Cardoner River the eyes of his understanding began to open and without seeing any vision, he understood and knew many things, as well spiritual things as well as things of faith. (autobiography 30)

During this period of introspection Ignatius decided to pursue an education, first elementary studies then university and finally a master's degree from College of Sainte-Barbe, University of Paris at the age of 43. He was ordained a Catholic priest and lived his life teaching about the spiritual process. His spiritual quest for better understanding of making the correct choices in ethical versus moral decisions and God's will. This information is included on his history to again inform that the process of spirituality is transformative for the purpose of changing and becoming more human working toward full potential. In 1534 Loyola, Francis Xavier and Diego

Laizez founded a new holy order while living in Rome. It was approved by Pope Paul III in 1540. They called it the Society of Jesus or better known as the Jesuits. Francis Xavier was younger and offered to travel the world as a missionary for the Jesuits. He went to India where he was very well received. He taught spiritual concepts and interacted is a positive way with members of the Buddhist spiritual groups in the countries he visited including Japan, Cambodia, Maluku Islands, Vietnam, Thailand Sri Lanka, Myanmar. There is a preponderance of evidence to indicate that while in India Xavier was credited for calling the Buddhist spiritual texts scripture. Buddhism and the ideas now presented as Buddhist spirituality owe much to the Jesuits missionaries in general from the 16 Century up until 1550 when the Jesuits for the most part where responsible for teaching many of the Buddhist Spirituality history in the various educational institutions in addition of course to Christian Doctrine. Francis Xavier was beatified and canonized as a Saint and now in the 21st Century continues to be respected and honored in India.

At the time of Loyola's death, the Jesuits had followers in Italy, Spain, Portugal, Germany, France, India, Congo and Ethiopia. Loyola wrote the structure and sent missionaries to many countries. The core of his program concluded that being highly educated all the way up to the university levels and graduate school can be an essential component on the journey to a greater spiritual understanding. Today the Jesuits have founded and manage a number of institutions around the world, including the 380 secondary schools and 190 colleges and 28 Jesuit colleges and universities and two theological centers in the USA.

On scruples: *"A person who desires to make progress in the spiritual life ought always to proceed in a manner contrary to that of the enemy. In other words, if the enemy seeks to make a soul lax, it should try try to make itself more sensitive. In the same way, if the enemy seeks to make a soul too sensitive, in order to entice it to an extreme, the soul should endeavor to establish itself staunchly in a correct mean and thus arrive at complete peace."* This is the middle position to all aspects of life. Saint Loyola was Beatified in 1609 by Pope Paul V and Canonized in 1622 by Pope Gregory XV.

APPLIED THEORY

"That both the giver and maker of spiritual exercises may be of great help and benefit to each other.... to put a good interpretation on a neighbor's statement than to condemn it. If one cannot interpret it favorable, one should ask how to the other means it...one should search out every appropriate means through which, by understanding the statement in a good way it may be saved."

Presupposition by Loyola

THE SPIRITUALITY OF FINDING A SOUL MATE IS SOMETIMES SYNCHRONICITY

...a fictional account of a wonderful spirituality devoid of expectation or materialistic pursuit and centered in equanimity...

It was a level of synchronicity when Samuel put his hand up to Anna's in the Vulcan mating ritual. As their fingers touched in a geometric complement, so did their souls. The Trekkie Vulcans control their emotionalism with logic which is well known. In the Star Trek series we learn that the Vulcans have the urge to court every seven years or perish. It is more of a symbolic end of existence that might occur for Samuel and Anna, but the positive thoughts of this narrator see a metaphor of similarity between the mating rituals of both the soulmates and the Vulcans. Pon farr comes complete with many of the emotional swings experienced by soulmate phases. Watching the Bounty episode confirms that for Vulcans biology overcomes rational control in a vast hormonal surge, the feverish compulsion to court, right alongside of the irritability and irrational emotions of anger at the loved one. The soulmate dance in fact only differs in one respect, which is the length of the courtship far exceeding the seven days, to the enlightenment and ultimate joy of the relationship.

An example that depicts no obvious causal relationship between events or series of messages that are leading the individual, but unknown to the individual at the same time. It can be very confusing until seen in retrospect. Carl Jung, the world-famous psychiatrist, coined the use of the word synchronicity as a concept during the early 1900s.

A young child requests piano lessons at age twelve. She promises to study hard and convinces the parents she will never need to be told to practice her lessons. Something about her intensity motivates her father to pay the local music teacher to provide instruction. The child's musical passion is combined with talent, but lessons are expensive, so they are put on hold. The wonderful woman who is her first teacher provides one final free lesson and teaches her prodigy to play Vivaldi's Four Seasons Le Quattro Stagioni as if she were a world class musician. They play Winter for Four Hands, Quattro. It is exhilarating and our young pianist memorizes the sheet music for a duet that will be a major part of her life. As the youngster exits the music studio after that last lesson she is met with a soft rain and can't for the moment decide if it is a tear running down her face at the disappointment of no future lessons, but the sun shines brightly and a small but magnificent rainbow appears.

The mother of our young musician in the making suggests she study the flute in the sixth grade where the lessons are free and the instrument can be rented. The point is made that learning to read music is the goal at this point anyway. The end result is a smashing blow to a young pianist-to-be but she complies and learns the basics of what we suspect will be a career in the world of music.

Fast forward to high school and the young teen who loved the piano has taught herself to read music, write lyrics and has, before age fifteen, written several original pieces. Her passionate flame for the piano now includes a part time job enabling her to pay for her own private lessons. Unfortunately, life and finances get in the way at about this point and divert all of her energy to the field hockey team that her dad assures her will result in a full athletic scholarship and free ride to college.

And so it was that on that one night the future half of a soulmate is sitting in her dorm with nothing but a dumb reality show to watch or accept the invitation of a sorority sister and attend a free concert. She opts for the concert, expecting the usual ear drum shattering music of a hard rock band with the only relief from the high decibels coming when the musicians proselytize their pet political rhetoric of the month. Much of that dribble being in opposition to her work ethic and family values.

The walk to the concert will take about fifteen minutes and there is a slight misty rain falling. She opts to walk quickly, allowing the rain to coat her face which elicits days, long ago, of puddle jumping as a child. The nimbus clouds break and just at that moment before cumulous puffs float in, there is a rainbow. She smiles as we all do at the sight of a magnificent rainbow and, thinking nothing more than how blessed her life was at that moment, she heads into the concert building.

The amphitheater is silent and only half full. The student feels the hair on the back of her neck stand at attention as the pianist takes his seat. It is a wonderful turn of events and she is thrilled that she attended. The young musician is totally in awe and she is breathless at the sight of both the musician and the man. He seems familiar, perhaps one of the guys who pops up in her many dreams. This man is muscular, blond, blue-eyed and brilliant as he plays his first piece. It is one she has played many times but as she listens she falls in love, with him, his musical expertise, his look. He is older and has a mature presence. She is lost in the chords and melody of her pianist, loving every moment. As he returns for one more piece she tenses, sitting at the edge of her seat as she hears and remembers the first time she also played Winter for Four Hands, Quattro.

In what seems like minutes the evening concert ends and, standing on her chair, she shouts, "Bravo!" along with many others in attendance. The pianist exits the stage and she feels a sense of remorse that she will never meet him or be able to express her appreciation for his gift.

The young woman and the pianist of this meaningful event will in fact meet again in several years and enter the next phase of a lifelong soulmate relationship complete with children, grand children, jobs at a prestigious school of music and all the joys and sorrows of the classic soul mate relationship. Oh yes… at their wedding they performed a piano duet of the song Vivaldi Four Seasons, bringing new meaning to the idea of "their song" played at most weddings.   Preparing the limo for the honeymoon departure the driver says look at that amazing rainbow….

d'ecclesis, from her novel "Twin Flame"

APPLIED THEORY

Draw a mandala by drawing a circle first, then a vertical and horizontal line, creating four quadrants with the circle. Draw a small circle in the center of the larger one, Create shapes around the center. A mandala is a circular spiritual symbol used and drawn daily by Carl Jung as he formulated the theory of synchronicity.

ZEN AS A SYSTEM OF SPIRITUAL ETHICS & MEDITATION

Zen as a spiritual path allows us to experience our essence, opening a portal to view life spontaneously. The meditative path is a journey toward the sacredness of existence. It is said we can all be serenely zen on a mountain during the idyllic vacation, but the true enlightenment is replicating that during the stress of our daily lives in the workplace, in family relationships and our internal anxiety with daily life. Zen is a Japanese division of Buddhist practice. It originated...Many years ago...approximately 2700 years past...

Who was this man we call Buddha and how did he formulate his ideas and philosophy known as the Noble Path? A view of his life's experiences and how they impacted to help form the concept of Middle Path Spiritual Existence:

Buddha was the son of Queen Maha Maya and King Suddhodana who owned the municipality of Kapilavastu in an area of India now known as Nepal. Late in life the queen realized she was pregnant and with great joy informed her husband. Maya wanted to go back to her parents because her baby was almost due. Since it was the custom in India for a wife to have her baby in her father's house, the king agreed. So, the King made the arrangements for his queen to travel in royal style. On the way to the Koliya country, the great procession passed a garden called Lumbini Park. This garden was near the kingdom called Nepal, at the foot of the Himalayan Mountains. It was very warm and Queen Maya decided to go wading into a lake. Shortly after that she went into labor and while holding the branches of a tree, she gave birth to son who would be named. Siddhartha Gautama.

The birth took place on a full moon which is now celebrated as Vesak, the festival of the triple event of Buddha's birth, enlightenment and death, in the year 623 BCE This date is still in question and subject to much debate. The times of Gautama's birth and death are uncertain: most historians in the early 20th century dated his lifetime as circa 563 BCE to 483 BCE but more recent opinion dates his death to between 486 and 483 BCE or, according to some, between 411 and 400 BCE However, at a symposium on this question held in 1988, the majority of those who presented definite opinions gave dates within 20 years either side of 400 BCE for the Buddha's death. These alternative chronologies, however, have not yet been accepted by all other historians.*

*Hans Wolfgang Schumann (2003). The Historical Buddha: The Times, Life, and Teachings of the Founder of Buddhism, p. xv. Motilal Banarsidass Publ. ISBN 8120818172

After the birth of her baby son, Queen Maha Maya immediately returned to Kapilavastu to present the King his son. The infant was given the name Siddhartha Gautama in Pāli: Siddhartha, meaning "he who achieves his aim". Seven days after her return home

Queen Maya died. Siddhartha was born in a royal Hindu family and many helped care for him. He was brought up by his mother's younger sister, Maha Pajapati.

The king was devastated and called for advice from his advisors to help him understand why the joyful birth of his son caused the death of his wife. The king also wanted to know what type of life his new child would have and how he should raise him, so he called for Asita a hermit who was ascetic and had great psychic powers. Asita predicted that the Prince Siddhartha of Kapilavastu would either become a great king, called a chakravartin or become a spiritual leader and Buddha.

The king did everything he could think of to be certain his son Prince Siddhartha would grow up prepared for a life following in his own footsteps and become a king of the municipality. The prince was taught archery and math and fighting skills as a young child but always showed signs of compassion and refused to hunt.

When he reached the age of 16, the king arranged the prince's marriage to a cousin of the same age named Yasodhara. It is said he did so because the future Buddha was so kind and gentle and the uncles suggested he needed a wife to make him more "manly". The young prince and princess enjoyed a charmed life so important to the future Buddha's story. It is during this time that Siddhartha's philosophy of life was formed. He lived in total luxury.

Of his luxurious life as a prince he states:

"I was delicate, excessively delicate. In my father's dwelling three lotus ponds were made purposely for me. Blue Lotuses bloomed in one, red in another, and white in the third. I used no sandwood that was not kasi. My turban, tunic, dress and cloak were all kasi. Night and day a white parasol was held over me so that I might not be touched by heat or cold, dust leaves or dew."

*"There were three palaces built for me-one for the cold season, one for the hot season, one for the rainy season. During the four rainy months, I lived in the palace for the rainy season, entertained by female musicians, without coming down from the palace. Just as in the houses of others, food from the husks of rice together with sour gruel is given to the slaves and workmen, even so, in my father's dwelling, food with rice and meat was given to the slaves and workmen". ** *

*A Manual of Buddhism", Narada,
1992, Kuala Lumpur, Malaysia

We begin to see a pattern of the future Buddha growing bored with the ostentatious lifestyle of his father. However, his father was a great King who treated all humans well in a time when that was not the norm. Prince Siddhartha's starts to question the meaning of life and what lies beyond the walls of Kapilavastu at about the same time Yaśodhara got pregnant after all those years.

According to the history, she gave birth to a son, named Rahula who was named by his father. It is interesting to note the meaning of the name Rahula - a soft fetter or chain.

Siddhartha is said to have spent twenty-nine years as a prince in Kapilavastu. Although his father ensured that Siddhartha was provided with everything he could want or need, Buddhist scriptures say that the future Buddha felt that materialism was not what gave his life meaning. The prince requested that his father permit him to enter the city on the other side of the wall. The prince went on a journey and saw old age for the first time.

When the prince saw the old man, he didn't know what was wrong with this man. It was the first time in his life that he had seen an old person.

The next sighting was of a man crying out in pain in a scream. This made the prince very sad. Channa who was Siddhartha's friend tried to explain that everyone in this world will eventually get sick, old and die. Buddha asks, 'Why does a man lie there so still, allowing people to burn him? It's as if he does not know anything.' Channa explained the man was dead. Channa explained that the happy men walking around smiling were monks seeking spiritual truths. The Buddha thought that perhaps he would like being a monk.

The prince felt very happy now and decided to become a monk. He walked until he was tired, then sat under a tree to think some more. As he was sitting under the cool shady tree, news came that his wife had given birth to a fine baby boy. Siddhartha felt the baby to be an impediment, Rahula has been born and he felt him to be an obstacle to leaving.

Siddhartha was determined to leave anyway so Channa prepared his horse and Siddhartha went to see his newborn son for the first time. His wife was sleeping with the baby beside her. The prince decided to go without waking them to finish what he was looking for and he felt that at some point he would return. Prince Siddhartha left his father's estate, took off his robes and cut his hair to two fingers breath. He became known as ascetic Gautama. He walked all over Northern Indian for almost six years fasting and seeking enlightenment.

Siddhartha decided to sit under a banyan tree to meditate, he was very weak. A young woman named Sujata saw him and offered sweet thick milk rice in a golden bowl. When he finished, he took the golden bowl and threw it in the river. He felt if this bowl floated upstream he would give up the path of asceticism. The golden bowl went upstream keeping in the middle of the river. He decided at that moment to sit and meditate until he was enlightened. After he sat for days and faced his demons, Buddha achieved enlightenment.

The first teaching ever given by Shakamuni Buddha was to five student monks in a deer park. The Buddha spoke of the Four Noble Truths he had discovered while struggling for enlightenment, these are the central teachings of Buddhism.

THE FOUR NOBLE TRUTHS

1. **Life means suffering**. During our lifetime we experience illness, injuries, failures, the aging process and finally death. There is suffering along the way as well as joy. Accepting the inevitable loss of our expectations that things will go smoothly almost perfect we realize that life has many degrees of suffering. The suffering is called, Duhka a nagging dissatisfaction.

2. **The origin of suffering is attachment and desire**. We all crave and cling to the materialistic things we desire such as wealth as a goal in and of a goal as itself, as well as attaching to transient imperfect pursuits of fame and popularity. The attachment is to impermanent things and living exists in an impermanent nature.

3. **The cessation of suffering is attainable**. The suffering we submit ourselves to can cease to exist by becoming dispassionate. Equanimity removes the suffering and allows us to maintain a dispassionate life devoid of the ups and downs. We become observers of life without the manic or depressed responses.

4. **There is a path to cessation of suffering**. The Path as described by the Buddha is called The Eight-fold Path to a middle place. It is living our lives without excessive self-

indulgence or asceticism. The Noble Eightfold Path as described by Siddhartha Gautama or historical Buddha helps us to understand a moral, ethical and meditative journey to live our lives learning to be content in the chaos. The entire middle path principles are inter-dependent in symbiotic relationship with each other.

The path is called the Eightfold Path and is presented here in its entirety.

THE STEPS OF THE EIGHTFOLD PATH

WISDOM

1. Right View or Understanding is to see things as they really are. We should stay in the present, being in the moment at all times.

2. Right Intention is to set intention to avoid anger, violence and desires. Not having thoughts of greed and anger.

MORALITY AND ETHICS

3. Right Speech

Avoid lying, gossip, harsh speech, slander and saying hurtful things.

4. Right Action is similar to the golden rule do no harm to others, no killing, no stealing, no over indulging, no excessive drugs or alcoholism, no intoxicating substances, no attention seeking. Not to destroy any life, not to steal or commit adultery. Jukai or Taking the Precepts in Buddhism structures right action.

5. Right Livelihood

Avoiding occupations that bring harm to oneself and others. Earn wealth legally and peacefully, no arms dealing, no prostitution, no raising animals for slaughter, no slave trade, no drug dealing, no just war, no abattoir, no executioner. However, Buddha was very clear it is not proper to tell anyone what they do is wrong.

MENTAL DISCIPLINE

6. Right Effort

Earnestly doing one's best in the right direction. Work on yourself to get rid of improper attitudes. This requires self-discipline.

7. Right Mindfulness

Always being aware and attentive. alive our lives in the moment and being mindful, when we are eating, just eat.

8. Right Concentration

To making the mind steady and calm in order to realize the true nature of things by meditating. All of the Buddhist meditations have value and should be practiced, kinhin-walking, zazen-shikantaza-seated TO ACHIEVE SATORI OR ENLIGHTENMENT.

Buddhists believe that following the Eightfold Path leads, ultimately, to a life free of suffering or Satori. Taking the Precepts is a ceremony in Buddhism where people commit to the principles of the Noble Path and the three pure precepts and the ten grave precepts.

THE THREE PURE PRECEPTS

1. Not Creating Evil
2. Practicing Good
3. Actualizing Good For Others

THE TEN GRAVE PRECEPTS

1. Affirm life; Do not kill
2. Be giving; Do not steal
3. Honor the body; Do not misuse sexuality
4. Manifest truth; Do not lie
5. Proceed clearly; Do not cloud the mind
6. See the perfection; Do not speak of others errors and faults
7. Realize self and other as one; Do not elevate the self and blame others
8. Give generously; Do not be withholding
9. Actualize harmony; Do not be angry
10. Experience the intimacy of things; Do not defile the Three Treasures

APPLIED THEORY

1. Explain what the practice of Zazen meditation is to your group
2. Give a minute of silence to have everyone set a clear and positive intention for the day's Zazen.
3. Open our third eye Chakra with light pressure in a circular fashion
4. Practice breathing as a warm up to meditation and prepare the body for a relaxed meditative state.
5. Use visualization to breath in and out to locate our "Garden of Energy"- 2 inches below the umbilicus.
6. Obtain proper Zazen posture- upright with shoulders back, proper Mudra, proper tongue placement, inhalation and exhalation thru the nose, and using the mind's eye for visualization.
6. Use the count if 4 for inhalation and the count of 6 for exhalation.
7. Use Thich Nhat Hahn's meditation for 12 minutes for beginners.
8. During meditation I repeat the count for the in and out breath and repeat what the practitioners should be visualizing repeatedly.

ETHICS MORALITY & SPIRITUAL WISDOM OF ASHOKA THE GREAT

"Amidst the tens of thousands of names of monarchs that crowd the columns of history, their majesties and graciousnesses and serenities and royal highnesses and the like, the name of Asoka shines, and shines, almost alone, a star. From the Volga to Japan his name is still honored. China, Tibet, and even India, though it has left his doctrine, preserve the tradition of his greatness." -H.G. Wells

Asoka (264 to 227 BC), one of the great monarchs of history, whose dominions extended from Afghanistan to Madras... is the only military monarch on record who abandoned warfare after victory. He had invaded Kalinga (255 BC), a country along the east coast of Madras, perhaps with some intention of completing the conquest of the tip of the Indian peninsula. The expedition was successful, but he was disgusted by what be saw of the cruelties and horrors of war. He declared, in certain inscriptions that still exist, that he would no longer seek conquest by war, but by religion, and the rest of his life was devoted to the spreading of Buddhism throughout the world. He seems to have ruled his vast empire in peace and with great ability. He was no mere religious fanatic. For eight and twenty years Asoka worked sanely for the real needs of men. More living men cherish his memory to-day than have ever heard the names of Constantine or Charlemagne.

-H. G. Wells, in The Outline of History (1920)

Ashoka built 84,000 Stupas to hold the relics of Buddha. The Stupas were also places where people could meditate. The people of entire Mauryan Empire where able to read his edicts carved in stone on fifty-foot pillars.

- Tolerance and understanding of all religions, as they are all pure of heart
- Digging of wells for irrigation and trees planted for shade
- More comfortable travel for both humans and animals
- No human or animal sacrifices permitted
- Building of hospitals and orphanages and medical care for all education of women
- Kindness to prisoners including a three day wait of appeal by relatives on behalf of the convicted
- Edicts of Ashoka a collection of 33 inscriptions on the pillars and cave walls so all could learn a better life under teachings and path of Buddhism
- Promoted vegetarianism
- Directed the third buddhist council
- All subjects as equals to each other

The Ashoka pillar at Sarnath has four lions and has become the national emblem of India.

Ashoka died at age 72 and most of his ideas and edicts were reversed by the rulers who came after him including the destruction of many cave edicts, pillars and stupas in war-torn modern-day countries. His ability to spread the Dharma did not die with him as evidenced by the practice of Buddhism in many of the countries where he sent Buddhist missionaries especially after his son Mahindra translated Buddhist Canon to the native languages.

APPLIED THEORY

Research and list Ashoka's major Rock Edicts or simply print out Ashoka's accomplishments listed above. Reflect on implementation of his ideas in your home country.

ART, CHANTING, POETRY, MUSIC

Haiku

Haiku in three short lines is a small poem that speaks volumes about how we think while viewing nature. We connect our true feelings of things in nature with a hint of the season and how we perceive it. The poet is motivated by the words in the haiku poem and feelings flow in free association. Haiku is seeing beauty in nature and then expressing it in the written word how we feel about it. Haiku takes place in the present, a moment in time.

Traditional haiku has some key elements:
Kigo, Kireji, Saikiki and Kiru.

Kigo is the traditional haiku reference to the season. The kigo alludes to the season for example spring might be young grass, cherry blossoms…. or frog peepers. Kigo are frequently in the metonyms or figures of speech that we use in place of the actual wording. It is the name of an association rather than its real name. An example would be Wall Street for financial services, Hollywood for the motion picture industry, the track for horse or dog racing and crown for the royal family, etc.

Kiru is a cutting in the poem and the most important part of haiku. It separates the juxtaposition in the haiku.

Kireji in traditional haiku always has a cutting word that divides the poem into sections with the purpose of each section helping to accent the understanding.

Many American haiku writers use a dash or ellipsis to substitute for kireji.

Saijiki is a reference pool from brainstorming a sort of dictionary for Kigo. It includes many trigger words from the seasons for use in the haiku.

The seasonal haikus contain many references: In Japan they are divided according to the dates each season begins and ends.

Saijiki Examples:

Spring - young love, pure, ethical, marriage, tranquil, serene, plow, herbs, silkworms, blossoms, azalea, buds, sprouts, nori, frogs

Summer - beach, sea, excess heat, sky blue, hot, south wind, fragrant breeze, evening downpour, thunder, drought, dripping waterfall, straw mats, rice planting, swimming, cutting grass, fireworks, airing, smog, cicada

Fall - loss, end of relationships, leaves changing, mysterious, autumn air, night chill, harvest moon, dew frost, mackerel clouds

Winter - snow, ice, no leaves, loss, NYE, short day, no leaves, fireplace, bonfire, hawk, wood burning stove, porridge, seven herbs, cold, freezing, windy

Styles for Writing Haiku

The most basic system to use when writing haiku is to ask questions and answer them in the poem. When writing haiku the writer simply answers the questions. The writer answers what the haiku is about, where it is taking place, which season is represented and perhaps even a time period. The writer can then organize the poem to obtain the desired effect.

Here is an example of the way Basho did it:

Blowing Stones
Along the road on Mount Asama
The autumn wind

The what in this poem would be the blowing stones. The where would be along the road on Mount Asama. The when would be in the fall due to the use of the words "the autumn wind". The simplicity of this style does make it the perfect place to start as a student of haiku. Like any haiku, what matters is the impact of the content.

Juxtaposition is very common in many haikus. It involves taking separate images and showing a relationship between them. There are many types of relationships that can be shown between distinct images. The haiku can take the images and show a contrast depending on the desired realization or understanding.

Here is an example of Basho expressing a similarity between two distinctly different things:

Felling a tree
And seeing the cut end -
Tonight's moon

Basho is expressing the similar look between the ring portion of a cut tree to the full moon.

Here is an example of contrast in a haiku written by Basho:

> *The winter sun –*
> *On the horse's back*
> *My frozen shadow*

In this haiku Basho expresses the contrast between the winter sun, which can give off slight relieving warmth, to the harshness of the cold winter. This also relates to how nothing in life is permanent. Even though it is winter there is slight warmth from the sun, however that sun may not last and the bitter cold will return.

Here is an example of an association haiku written by Basho:

This autumn –
Why am I growing old?
Bird disappearing among clouds

In this haiku Basho is associating aging and losing his youth to the fall where things tend to die off and go dormant. The birds disappearing can be associated to his youth leaving him.

One exciting way to write haiku is by the suspense of what I call crescendo much like … "coming next on the news". This style is used at night when all the TV watcher is interested in is the weather report but the meteorologist slowly gives us small parts of the forecast saving the best for the last few minutes of the broadcast. Using this style the main subject of the haiku is gradually exposed throughout the poem. It is mystery being revealed. With each line the poem builds to inform us of the final subject matter. An example of the crescendo style written by Basho:

Autumn moonlight –
A worm digs silently
Into the chestnut

The overall image is nothing more than a worm eating away at some chestnut, but it is the way Basho creates the scene in the reader's mind that makes these types of haiku so effective. Basho

104

paints a scene of a full moon on an autumn night, then leads into the worm digging silently. Most readers would assume the worm would be eating dirt, but then Basho reveals that the worm is digging into a fine wood.

The key to writing unveiling haiku is to create a sense of mystery and that something is coming next. Treat the haiku like a strange puzzle. Start with a vague scene, provide a small detail, and then finish the puzzle with the final piece.

I like the general to the specific approach in haiku which involves starting with a broad scene and focusing down into a small point or element of the scene. The specific to the general involves the exact opposite starting with a single point or element of a scene and expanding outward to the entire broad scene.

Here is an example of the general to the specific technique written by Basho:

> *Spring rain*
> *Leaking through the roof*
> *Dripping from the wasps' nest*

Basho starts very broad with the imagery of a spring rain shower. He then focuses in to the rain leaking through a roof. He focuses even further now to the rain water dripping from a wasps' nest. Basho went from a broad image all the way to a single element of the nest. This shows the beauty of nature from a broad scene all the way down to an intricate detail. Life exists on all scales large and small.

Here is an example of a specific to the general haiku written by Basho:

> *A crow*
> *Has settled on a bare branch*
> *Autumn evening*

Basho starts with a focused image of a crow. It is very simple and detailed. Basho then focuses out to the crow now sitting on a bare branch. He expands even further now to the image of an autumn evening. Basho started with the basic image of a crow and builds to an image of a vast autumn night scene where the reader envisions leaves fluttering in a cool fall breeze with a full moon.

There is a style of writing haiku that is imbedded in its very origins. Shiki liked this when he learned it from Basho and suggested that we write from a realistic perspective exactly what we were experiencing in our lives. How simple is that?

Here is an example of the basic realism style by Basho:

> *A snowy morning –*
> *By myself*

Chewing on dried salmon

This haiku accurately depicts a morning experience of Basho's. We have all had those mornings where we are gazing out the window munching on something with that same contented feeling of "ok let's start this day" and proceeded to do just that after we finished our bacon!

One of my personal favorite American haiku writers is Richard Wright. He used realism of activities in this haiku:

In the falling snow
A laughing boy holds out his palms
Until they are white

Haiku by d'ecclesis:

On Sacred Mountain
Hirayama Style Castle
Texting Under Trees

APPLIED THEORY

How To Write Your First Haiku

Go hiking in a beautiful natural setting. Take a pad and pencil and a smart phone for pictures if you have one. Stop near the stream and watch the snow melting and how it causes the water to rush faster. Photograph it or even better make a video. Take notes and how it makes you feel and what thoughts are entering your mind. Write how you feel and what you see at that moment.

Log the sensory input.
Include: SMELLS, SOUNDS, EMOTIONS, SIGHTS, COLORS

Write a list of key words coming into your mind. They might include, gloomy, sweltering, aroma, salty, taste buds. Now you become the poet. Write two lines from the experience without form. Just write it.

Return now to your desk to fine tune the poem with style and form. View everything again, the key words and the pictures. Write one more line that has nothing to do with the first two lines of your poem. Now, using your fingers count the syllables in the first two line omitting or adding as needed to bring the poem to standard haiku form. (I use my fingers): **5 ~ 7 ~ 5**

Music: Meditation Without Meditating

Few things in this world are more expressively powerful than music – it includes physical, emotional, and spiritual components. The act of creating music helps enhance focus and concentration, teaching how to truly listen. It is an easy way to separate from conscious thought, shutting off the mental chaos of a long workday, being a conduit for inward focus.

A performing musician knows that when onstage, the connection with the audience is a one-of-a-kind encounter, where inward focus and outward connection can be felt at the very same time. In other words, it is a meditative act crossing paths and intertwining with a communal spirit. The experience is breathtaking and indescribable –a spirituality, that, by definition, is impossible to define. The concentration that is necessary to progress to better levels of musicianship is very similar to that of meditation, yet for many, it is easier to attain. After all, many will be better able to bring straying focus back to a chord progression than to breathing. Not only will the ability to truly listen be enhanced, but the ability to "stop listening" will also develop. Many will agree that shutting off the mental faucet is one of the most difficult skills to master. Best of all, playing music is fun; a sentiment that isn't shared by all those who have attempted conventional meditation.

Social interaction through music is a spiritual connection. Playing a musical instrument gives you a life-long pursuit for which you can

set and achieve both short and long-term goals, but rarely arrive at true mastery. It is for this reason that playing music becomes so valuable. With no pre-conceived end point in mind, it provides a tool that develops the ability to live in the moment and enjoy the journey rather than focus solely on the horizon. Not only will it result in a lifetime of near-meditative relaxation, but playing an instrument also opens up many opportunities for social interactions with like-minded people.

Musical ability affords one not only individual freedom to explore creativity in solitude if so desired, but also the connections to a huge community of thoughtful, creative people who share a similar passion. Learning to selflessly contribute to the creative concept of a group is a type of fulfillment that is unique to this particular form of artistic expression. Neither writers, nor painters have the same opportunities that musicians have to experience growth on inter-personal levels. The ensemble dynamic of music can instill the ability to generate selfless contributions within a group of people. This can easily translate to better relationships in other areas of life.

A chant is a spiritual portal produced by singing reciting tones. It is used by many religious and spiritual communities as a path toward spiritual development. The sacred chanting brings one closer to higher self. The Vedic mantra chanting beginning and ending in OM is widely used in the more modern Transcendental Meditation. It is a process of faith and repetition of the Mantra. With Zen Buddhists chanting prepares the mind for meditation. The use of the Heart

Sutra for example chanted before each Zazen expresses Sunyata. Roshi John Daido Loori references the great Zen Master Dogen.

The Christian Gregorian chant is a form of monophonic chanting from the 9th Century sung in 12 modes. It is widely listened to as a spiritual experience in the twenty first century.

Indigenous people use music and specifically drumming in spirit practice. In addition to creating a cohesive community from groups who practice Shamanic drumming to the continent of Africa where percussions are used in various ceremonies in many villages the amazing mind body spirit connection is enhanced.

NATIVE AMERICAN SPIRITUAL COMMUNICATION: CALLING THE CIRCLE

The learning of new concepts from ancient techniques that have proven to be of great value has us take a look at Calling the Circle or using a talking stick. The Circle is an interactive and egalitarian technique with includes a spiritual exchange developed by Native Americans. It enhances communication skills with a structure and nearly eliminates the stress produced by speaking publicly. No one has an obligation to speak if they don't want to. They can defer to the person sitting next to them.

The Talking Stick – sometimes called a "speaker staff" or a "talking piece" is an object that promotes spirituality during a discussion. In a tribal council circle, a talking stick is passed around from member to member allowing only the person holding the stick to speak. This permits all those present at a council meeting to be heard, especially those who tend to be introverted. Talking "lean" precludes the people who talk on forever from dominating the discussion. Speaking and listening from the heart are always part of the process and an excellent rule of speaking spontaneously after receiving the stick prevents the group from "thinking" about their responses while others are talking. The technique therefore has four precepts or rules: Talking lean, talking spontaneously, listening from the heart and speaking from the heart creating a truly spiritual exchange.

The stick is a "Talking Stick" has been used by Native Americans for years. The Talking Stick has been used in large corporations emulating tribal councils. The "Talking Stick" allows both space and time for the person holding the stick to make a point, to have their say, to be heard.

It is not just a talking stick, there is a flip side, it is also a listening stick for all those in its presence at a meeting, or "Calling the Circle". There are some additional rules, like time limits.

We need to "talk lean", get to the point, be both quick and concise, but we also need to be attentive and open to the person who is holding that stick. Well, how does this process work then? One by one, we try or take a "pass" not wishing to add anything at the time and pass the stick to the person next to us in clock-wise order. We sit in our small circles, holding the stick, looking at it, turning it and feeling it in our hands, learning to compose our thoughts before talking. We begin to speak, slowly, quietly, concisely with the refined words well thought out and pared down to the bone. The others at the table without the Talking Stick are clearly present and perhaps for the first time, listening to the words being provided by another person talking. They are learning not to think of what to say in response or what we wish to add to the topic at hand. This is not always easy, learning to speak, learning to be quiet, learning to listen...to really listen, to another's point of view. The Circle is called and we begin. The topic: "What scares you past or present?" This is an excellent starting point.

First, the intention is set to explore a specific topic – so rather than "how is everyone doing?" it might be more like, "What is the one thing that has been on your mind this week about your relationships with other people?" Then, we teach it is imperative that we listen to each other so it is suggested that no one formulates what they plan to say while another is speaking. The style is extemporaneous speaking. Time limits are used as guidelines so that one person does not dominate the entire session.

Calling the Circle is a unique way of communicating which most have never used before. Why a circle? In the 12th Century, the culture of Indigenous people called Haudenosaunee who lived around 1142 CE The Haudenosaunee people of the longhouse came from six tribes: Seneca, Onondaga, Oneida, Cayuga, Mohawk and Tuscarora. They met in a Grand Council Circle and after lighting their fire exchanged ideas and opinions and formed a democratic government. In addition to the Swiss and Icelandic cultures, it is one of the oldest democracies, but the techniques were a spiritual ritual of the tribes. There is documentation to indicate that during some circles not one word was ever spoken, the spiritual nature of the group predominated.

The study of this Iroquois Society reveals that women gained a huge role in government thru the use of the Grand Council. Women existed as equal partners and owned property, horses, homes and farms. When the man entered into marriage he lived with the woman's family. All ties of the children were traced through the mother's family lines and their spiritual rituals. The Chief's sister even selected the next chief after a meditative event. The female circle used men as runners between council and had the power to demote warriors and take away their symbol of power, the antler headpiece. Simply put, the Grand Council, where seventy-five percent of the men and the women had to agree, created spiritual communication skills between civilized groups of people, facing each other in an open circle with a fire in the middle. During a Circle the participants would sometimes sit in silence for hours only to know the answer and ruling of the majority. This level of spirituality exists in higher levels of consciousness. The fire in the middle represented future generations.

The term "Calling The Circle" originated with Christina Baldwin in her 1998 book of the same name. The use of a talking piece in combination with a circle of group interaction emulates the early tribes. It is frequently mentioned by participants as the most an emotionally liberating event. This ancient practice establishes itself in modern day because of the ever-increasing need for better face-to-face communication.

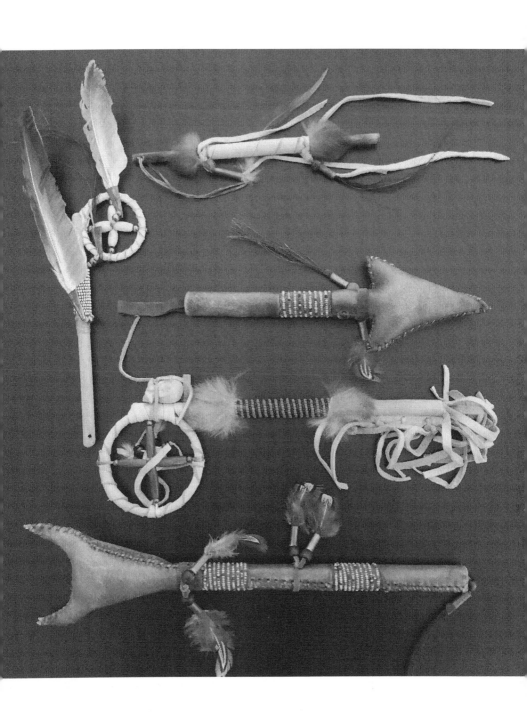

APPLIED THEORY

Select a talking stick, a topic and find a small group interested in this practice. Start by explaining the format of "talk lean," talk spontaneously, speak and listen from the heart chakra and only while holding the talking piece. Select a spiritual leader to set the tone and rules of order so confidentiality is maintained. Include the lovely Jewish tradition of a sacred guest by placing an empty extra pillow in the group. The spirituality of holding the staff is found in the Islamic traditions and a talking piece was used by Achilles and Agamemnon as told in The Iliad to help find middle ground in dispute.

MODERN REIKI HEALING FOUNDED IN SPIRITUAL PRINCIPLES OF THE REIKI MASTER

There are several obstacles which preclude spirituality. Included in the list are hate, fear-based emotions, indecision, immaturity and arrogance. Usui Reiki principles from Japan serve as a structure to move past these obstacles. The principles do not use the words I, me, mine because they are taken from affirmations that believe in egolessness.

JUST FOR TODAY, DO NOT ANGER.

Place your hands over your eyes, what the eyes don't see the heart doesn't grieve about. Anger might be an evolutionary emotion that has survival value because it keeps you from being taken advantage of from people who want what you have. It is a form of aggression. Release the need for this immature emotion that served generations in the past, but is no longer needed in our civilized and more compassionate world. Realize that it causes a fight or flight reaction and increased cortisol which decreases quantity and quality of life. Visualize a kinder gentler reaction to all of the various triggers that result in what we call anger. See yourself getting cut off on the highway and gently accepting the intrusion by dropping back and decreasing speed and letting him go, letting go of the anger that hurts only you. Practice equanimity. If we learn not to anger we will be able to show gratitude and showing gratitude to all living things will result in anger not being able to arise. It is imperative to practice what we say we believe.

JUST FOR TODAY, DO NOT WORRY

Worry shuts down the sacral chakra and stops abundance from flowing into your life. When you stop worrying abundance returns.

Create healthy imprints that come in the form of saying something, doing something or even thinking something. Place hands over temples, the temples are related to the active sides of the brain, therefore using this principle indicates balance of thoughts and thinking. Worry use to prepare us by anticipating the physical threats of the dinosaur in pursuit. Worry is excessive concern. It has evolved in us to prepare for the potential dangers. Worry about past choices that can't be changed and future calamities that may or may not happen has deleterious affect on our bodies. Visualize a feeling of trust and serenity. See your teen-ager charge the sea with her surfboard and think good thoughts, know that she will soon stand and ride that glorious wave all the way to the shore. Believe in her and accept that biting your nails until bloody will not result in an injury free ride. See the smile on her face and the joy in her aura as she glides in joy and feel pride in her athleticism and training without a care in the world.

HONOR YOUR PARENTS, TEACHERS AND ELDERS

Healing the relationship with parents and elders is more about gaining insight into how those interactions have created imprints in our youth, that to this day cause distress especially with people in authority who sent us messages of following their rules or withdrawing love and affection. Place your hands over back of head. Honor all parents and elders with the full understanding that they did their best job. Reflect back to the structure and discipline they provided to keep us safe and out of harm's way. To teach us basic facts and general funds of knowledge. We will journey back in time and visualize the many times mom told us to put on our coat when it was cold outside. The mountain of snow was so inviting and we knew best and wanted to just jump in without all those hats and coats. Without fail we were told we would get sick and the cold and fever followed the joy of the snowball fight. As we got older, we really knew it all and told the parents we could not possibly get sick without the coat because germs caused colds. But the elders knew best and the attack of 15 degrees on our immune system did in fact correlate to the colds and the excellent advice of wearing protective clothing. Visualize yourself interacting with the elders in a more trusting and respectful way and the love that creates.

EARN YOUR LIVING HONESTLY

Place your hands over the throat, the area of communication. Visualize yourself as a young child in a class of faith-based study. The regular teacher is absent and the substitute is a jolly man who loves to be teaching that day. He steps up to the lectern and has your undivided attention because from his first words you know this is your first exposure to spirituality. He begins by saying work to your fullest potential whatever the job, feel good about your work and give it 100% every hour of the day. Earn your living honestly and ethically and give it all you have. Do not complain or resent or anger. Do your work, single task and be paid for an honest day of labor. Part of your work is your attitude and spiritual path. End your day with prayer and or meditation.

SHOW GRATITUDE TO ALL LIVING BEINGS

Place your hands over your heart the area associated with love...

Start this visualization with the smallest living being, bacteria, living in our intestines that make nutrients and process toxins and enable us to digest and for them we are grateful. Breathe in the oxygen produced by plants and trees and yes go out and hug them! See the honeybees pollinating our plants and the joy of our companion dogs and cats jumping on our heads early on a Saturday morning. Hear Grandma Lea saying if you have your health you have everything, We can hear her if I concentrate on those words and then rejoice in the value of that statement.

Value life and be grateful for what you have no matter how much or how little. Express your gratitude by writing a gratitude list weekly.

APPLIED THEORY

Start your day with gratitude for what you do have. As your feet touch the floor, set an intention to ground yourself. Reiki has formal precepts or principles to set intention: Just for today: do not anger; do not worry; honor your parents, teachers and elders; earn your living honestly; show gratitude to all living beings.

Eco Spirituality

Last, but not least, saving the best for last! Many of the worlds ancient religions and spiritual practices involve voluntary acts of asceticism which is the avoidance of all forms of indulgence. They do this to reach spiritual goals for themselves and to have a positive effect on their communities. Both Siddhartha and Loyola spent years — decades in fact — living ascetic lives on their respective spiritual quests. They put in hours of meditation and or prayer practice. They worked toward a higher consciousness. They were willing to practice the self-discipline needed to achieve their spiritual goals. This notion should not be lost on us in modern times. For example, it is common knowledge that making dietary changes can improve our own health but also the health of our planet and the long-term future for our children and their children.

A simple concept such as reducing unhealthy foods in the diet can help reduce greenhouse gases and lower cholesterol. The health of the individual would be affected in a positive way and reduce the likely consequences of metabolic syndrome. From the perspective of spirituality perhaps the occasional use of foods known to be less than healthy is a good start, a once a month beef burger rather many each week, rather than learning to rely entirely on comforts to cope with life's difficulties. This can start with a simple exercise, found as the last suggested exercise in this book which in turn may create a habit and become a permanent part of your lifestyle.

Once you have had a chance to process the benefits of a simplistic life and changed a few habits you will enjoy all the benefits of better quantity and quality of life. It may not readily appear that one person can make a difference but in historical review, we know most spiritual figures began by setting an example starting alone often in the face of resistance and inspired not only their communities but generations thousands of years later. This is evident by the selection of spiritual leadership traditions from BCE, but also the nailing of Martin Luther's Ninety-Five Thesis in 1517 to the door of the Wittenberg Castle Church, resulting in totally reforming Christianity.

If each of us can lead by example, we will improve our own lives and demonstrate to others the impact they can make by doing the same. This is step one away from the self-obsessed behavior so common in society as we acknowledge and take action to realize that the time is now to prioritize the highest consciousness of the global community.

This has historically been the goal of spiritual practices; to better ourselves and those around us. Do one thing each day to move faster through the stages of maturity from the competitive warrior to the spiritual compassionate beings.

"Do not seek to follow in the footsteps of the wise. Seek what they sought. Seek not the paths of the ancients; seek that which the ancients sought"

Matsuo Basho

About the Author

Nora D'Ecclesis is an American bestselling non-fiction author and Haiku poet. Her international #1 bestseller "*The Retro Budget Prescription*" held the top kindle book downloads in business/self help for over a year. Nora is a graduate of Kean University of New Jersey with post graduate degrees in administration and education. She has a long history of presenting events, retreats and seminars focused on wellness and stress reduction techniques.

Nora's published non-fiction include Amazon #1 bestseller "*Haiku: Natures Meditation*" and paperbacks/ebooks on topics such as time management, guided visualizations, gratitude/equanimity, journaling and zen meditation.

In June, 2017 she added novelist to her list with the publication of "*Twin Flame*" written with her Co-Author, William R. Forstchen who is a New York Times #1 bestselling novelist. *Twin Flame* is a novella about a man meeting, courting and marrying his soulmate. Nora defines the holistic concept of twin flames in relationships. It is a blending of views about faith, love and perseverance from a universal spiritual perspective. The narration includes insights from Nora's expertise in Zen, Meditation and Reiki. The book embraces the concept that there is a higher plan for everyone and that twin flames are created long before birth.

44381013R00077

Made in the USA
Middletown, DE
06 May 2019